How To Learn a Foreign Language

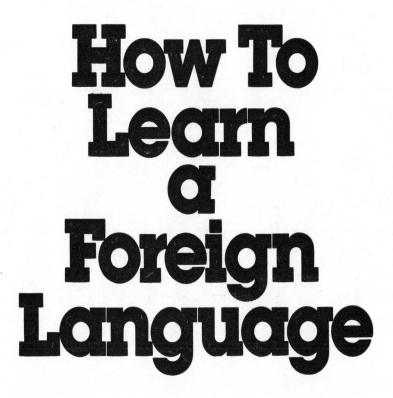

by Graham E. Fuller

BARNES & NOBLE BOOKS
NEW YORK

I dedicate this book to my family which
has shared with me so much of my life overseas:

Prue, Samantha, Melissa and Luke.

TABLE OF CONTENTS

GETTING
STARTED

INTRODUCTION

This book is for those of you who have never studied a foreign language before. And it is for those of you who have already had one painful experience with a foreign language and who hope to do better at it this time.

I'd like to pass along to you all the tips that it took me years of study in many different languages to learn. These tips all by themselves won't teach you a language—but they will help you to learn one.

And I want to teach you something about what foreign languages are all about—how languages work and how to approach this very special learning challenge. As you'll see, learning a foreign language—any foreign language—will be different from any other kind of study you have ever done.

I have had to study a great many languages over the past years. Fortunately, I've always liked languages. And since I've lived overseas in many different countries, I've had to learn quite a number of them just to do my job properly. Between job requirements and curiosity about languages—and a good bit of language work in college as well—I've studied to one extent or another more than a dozen of them, including Latin, Greek, Russian, Chinese, Arabic, Persian, Turkish and numerous European languages. In other words, I've been through it all, lots of times. My aim is to make the process as easy as possible for you, whatever your own language goal may be.

If you really like foreign languages, that's great. It will only make your task easier.

But this book isn't just for people who like languages. It's for those of you who have to learn a language for one reason or another. You might come to enjoy the process, but your goal is a practical one. And just because your goal is a practical one doesn't mean that the effort required to reach it can't be interesting—and even fun as well.

The main reason I've written this book is that I remember a lot of needless suffering the first time that I went through the process back in high school French. I had a friendly teacher who loved French—and he even knew how to teach. But there were hundreds of things about how to understand the *process of learning a language* that neither he nor anybody else ever told me. As a result I had to learn it the hard way, by trial and error, puzzling it out. It's that kind of inefficient, counter-productive work that I'd like to spare you.

But let's get one thing straight right away. Learning *any language* involves a lot of hard work. True, some languages are easier than others for English speakers. But any foreign language is going to require using a *whole range of different skills* that you may never have thought about before. This book will describe how to approach studying a foreign language and will outline the necessary skills. Then it will show you how to use them.

If you're lucky, you'll turn out to be one of those people who has a "knack" for languages. We often hear somebody say that Good Old So-and-So is "gifted" at learning languages. Or that somebody's cousin went to Mexico and "picked up" Spanish in a few months. In fact, no one has ever been able to decide just what it is that makes one person better at learning a language than another. Is is brains? Absolutely not. I've known a lot of people who are terrific at learning languages who don't know enough to come in out of the rain. And I've known a lot of people who are very smart— excellent at all sorts of academic work—who never get to be terribly good at a foreign language no matter how hard they try. Other people claim that it may be related to a sense of logic. Still others think that if you have a "musical ear" you will be better at languages. But nobody has ever convincingly demonstrated that these are key factors, either.

But if you turn out *not* to have a "knack" for languages—don't worry about it. And don't be discouraged. As you will see, learning a foreign language is like anything else in this world. If you are interested in accomplishing your goal, and if you devote a fair amount of attention to it, you'll succeed. But what else can make a difference?

Curiosity may have killed the cat, but it will certainly help you in languages. There are lots of fascinating aspects about foreign languages, from the people who speak them to the cultures they live in. Be prepared to learn some really interesting things. Get into the whole experience and ask questions about the culture you are studying and what makes the people tick. You may want to learn about a people anyway. Language is one of the keys.

An ability to imitate, to mimic, and to play a role will come in handy in your language work. You can't be shy about trying out your new language. Everybody makes some dumb mistakes in speaking. It's par for the course. Just laugh it off and keep on plowing ahead.

Above all, a sense of enthusiasm will make a big difference. As you read through the pages and chapters to come, keep in mind that you're heading into a brand new kind of learning adventure unlike anything you've ever studied before. Enjoy it. And try to have some fun as you go. You'll be pleasantly surprised at how much easier the job will be.

CHAPTER ONE

HOW TO USE THIS BOOK

Chances are you will have a very good language teacher. And the chances are that this teacher will be very skilled at teaching you French, Spanish, Hebrew, Bulgarian, Burmese, or whatever language you happen to be learning.

This book is designed to pave the way for your teacher—and, of course, for you. In the pages to come you will learn what foreign languages are, how they work, why they are different from English, and in what ways. Most of all, you will learn how to *think about* a foreign language, how to be prepared for what's coming, and how to approach it, using the techniques that have worked best for me over the years.

Keep in mind that this book is not supposed to *teach* you Spanish, Russian, Japanese, or any other specific language. I leave that to the experts whose classes you'll be sitting in. They know what they're doing and will do it well. This book will *prepare* you for the extraordinary experience of learning a foreign language so that your actual classes won't come as too much of a surprise to you and so you can start right off knowing what to expect and how to study.

To use this book effectively, first read it through from beginning to end. Don't take notes, and don't worry about memorizing anything at all. Your objective is merely to get the feel of what it takes to learn any foreign language—of what sorts of skills are involved and of what sorts of study techniques work best. When you've finished reading this book, you will be ready to begin learning whatever foreign language you've chosen to study.

Remember—this is a handbook. So keep it handy and refer back to it often as you begin learning your chosen language. Use this book to supplement whatever you learn in class, and to remind yourself of the best techniques for practicing the specific language skills— pronunciation, vocabulary, conversation, grammar, and so forth—that your instructor will be teaching in class. By reading this book now, and then referring back to it as you go, you'll find it easier to get started and, then, easier to make progress.

Think of this as a book about how to go on a safari. After all, I'm not going to take you on the safari— your real guide awaits you in your class. But I can tell you what it's like to go on a safari and how to prepare for it in the best way possible.

Now you are about to embark on a remarkable experience—a safari into the mind and culture of a new people—in a way that you have never done before. **Bon voyage! Gute Reise! Shchastlivogo puti! Yi lu ping an! Rihla sa'ida! Yolunuz açık olsun!**

In other words—Have a good trip!

CHAPTER TWO

WHY DO I NEED A FOREIGN LANGUAGE?

If you are able to read this book you are already a lucky person. Why? Because you are able to speak and read English—the one language that is known and spoken by more people internationally than any other in the world. That means that just by growing up in an English-speaking country you are part of a huge group of people who can already communicate with one another. If you had grown up, say, in Finland or Mongolia or Fiji, you would be speaking a language that hardly anyone else in the world knows, or ever studies. People who live in countries like that absolutely have to study a foreign language—probably English—if they are ever going to travel or do anything outside their own small country. But you don't have to do that. You already have learned fluently what millions and millions of other people in the world have to spend hundreds—probably thousands—of hours learning. In fact, a pretty good case can be made that if you already speak English you don't need to learn a foreign language at all to function quite well in this world. But then, there are some good reasons why you don't need more than a high school education to get along in this world, either. We don't go to college just because it is essential to getting along in life. We go because there is also tremendous value in learning something more, training our minds and broadening our exposure to new things in the world. This may sound vague—and perhaps it is. But it just isn't always possible to put a clear dollar sign on everything we do. But for those of you who want some concrete reasons for going through the effort to learn a foreign language, here are some of them:

—A foreign language is a credential just as a degree in chemistry is—it's worth something on your resumé.
—Knowing another language allows you to operate in a bigger world than the one defined by your native language.
—Your foreign contacts will be favorably impressed by your seriousness of purpose in understanding their country and dealing with them.
—A foreign language opens the door to a foreign culture. It will open your eyes to the outside world.
—When you learn a foreign language, you learn a lot more about your own language.
—You'll have a lot of fun along the way. Really, you will.

In America we live in a huge country—a continent really—where we share a common language and a common culture. But we also have to live and function in a world where a lot of people do things very differently than we do. Whether or not we like all of the ways they do things, we still have to live in the same world and deal with them. That's what questions of foreign policy, for example, are all about: figuring out what people in other countries are likely to do, why, and how best to deal with them.

What does this have to do with language? Two things: If you can learn a foreign language well, you gain a great deal of access to that country. You can read its newspapers and magazines, listen to its television programs, talk to a greater variety of its people, and really understand them first hand. But more important, even if you never learn the foreign language really well, *you can still learn an amazing amount just from having worked at it for a limited period.* Learning a language is like getting inside somebody's mind. You start to learn a little more about how they think and express themselves.

The Japanese have made interesting comments about foreigners learning their language. Japanese are likely to be very complimentary to a foreigner who has learned some Japanese and is willing to try it out. But Japanese also say that they get a little nervous on those more unusual occasions when they meet a foreigner who speaks Japanese fluently, like a native. Why? They say they feel that the foreigner has learned too much about them, that he has gotten inside their culture and life too deeply. It's an invasion of their privacy.

Being able to understand someone who is speaking in his native language gives us the "flavor" of that person. Have you ever watched a comedian or an actor who uses some kind of regional accent to portray a personality? Like a hillbilly, or a cowboy, or a black musician, or a New England fisherman? By hearing the accent and the words and expressions that he uses, you get a strong feeling for his personality. We laugh or enjoy his performance because we feel we understand the personality or the type by hearing him speak in his "native language."

If you can learn something about how a foreigner expresses his thoughts, you are a great deal closer to getting into that culture than you ever were before. It's almost like learning a "secret code" into another culture. After all, one's native language is one of the closest and dearest things to a person. Not for nothing do we call it "the mother tongue."

A person's mother tongue, by the way, has a hold that is almost impossible to shake off. For instance, no matter how fluent we become in another language, we will nearly always continue to use our native language for the rest of our life in counting and doing math calculations in our head. During World War II anti-Nazi resistance forces in Europe believed the enemy was sending in spies to report on resistance activities; individuals would show up claiming to be Norwegian or Dutch when in fact they were Germans well-trained in one of those languages. The real test was to ask them to solve a math problem in long division—out loud. If a person was not a native speaker he usually had extreme difficulty in doing math out loud in a language other than his own native one. That kind of math error would often cost someone his head.

By learning a foreign language, you are in a way getting into the mind of that Frenchman, that Russian, or that Chinese. You are starting to share with him the way he "dresses" his own thoughts and expressions—in linguistic clothes very different than your own. You suddenly realize that we English-speakers have *our own* odd ways of saying and expressing things too. You start to learn that there is no "normal" or "right" way to say things, and that our way is no more "natural" than any other way.

This idea seems hard to accept. On our own continent we are surrounded by American English, so much so that some people even have a hard time accepting that the British speak the way they do. Mark Twain once remarked that he was sure that if you were to suddenly shake an Englishman awake at night he would forget—and talk like an ordinary American.

Knowing something about foreign languages is also an important experience in preparing you for your first trip abroad, whether you are just travelling or intend to set up a household. If you've struggled a little bit with a foreign language, you're going to be a lot more sensitive to the problems that foreigners have in speaking English to you.

Moreover, many foreigners will be grateful for any effort you make to learn their language. They know it represents hard work on your part and see it as a compliment to themselves. Even if you learn just enough of a language for basic social purposes, it will be time well invested. For a business executive it can be especially important, suggesting a more serious business interest and longer-term approach than somebody casually drifting through.

Even small gestures can have their rewards. I remember when my wife was approached by a shoe-shine boy in Istanbul the first day after we had moved to Turkey. At that stage my wife had learned enough Turkish to say "No thank you, I don't need it." The boy was so astonished that a foreigner could respond in his own language that he reached over and kissed my wife's hand. In later years her ability to pass the time of day in Turkish earned her a warm and regular welcome and a good number of friends among the merchants in Istanbul's Covered Bazaar.

Language study also helps you learn things about your own language that you never knew before, simply because you start to make comparisons between your language and the new one. I think I learned more about English grammar from studying foreign languages than I ever did from years of English in school. I never saw the point of learning what a "direct object" or a "prepositional phrase" was, until I suddenly had to learn how to express one in a foreign language. And only then did I really start to understand what it was in English.

A last good reason to study a foreign language is that the whole process can be fun. I'm not saying that it won't be hard work and, yes, a good bit of drudgery too. But you can also have a lot of laughs along the way.

Some of the fun comes from laughing at yourself. Trying to wrap your mouth around some foreign sound or phrase is funny, although it can be humbling too. You have to shed some of your own self-importance and your worries about dignity if you really want to make progress. And in some ways you make progress without really realizing it. You begin to learn how to think in an entirely new way—and to learn that there are many different ways to think in this world other than "our way."

Now a new dimension has been added to your life. You start being conscious of another culture which in turn enriches your own life. You start getting more and more interested in that country and its people, its food, its music and its novels and short stories. You find that a trip there takes on a whole new meaning. Every facet of life there becomes interesting to you— not just the monuments and the museums. Like that first trip to Paris after you have started to learn French:

-The cab driver takes you into town and unloads his view of life on you, suddenly emerging as a rich personality, reflecting all sorts of pithy views on life in France; things they don't tell you about in the history books.

-The ice-cream woman on the street sells you a cone of French vanilla, but in the process also corrects your French grammar, as only a Parisian would.

-You suddenly find yourself reading a political slogan scrawled on a wall. Moreover, you discover that it's a great thrill; you feel you have broken through to the new culture—if only in a small way.

After a while the language you are studying will itself take on a new personality. You will come to associate it with the whole range of experiences you have had. The mere sound of the language will bring back a series of memories and feelings. You are getting hooked by the language, and it has already become a new part of you. In short, you have discovered a new world.

CHAPTER THREE

TEACHING YOUR MOUTH NEW TRICKS

You think you know how to talk? Sure you do, but only in a limited way. You know *one* way to talk, but there are dozens of different ways to make sounds that you never thought of. Remember when you were a child how you used to imitate the sound of trucks, airplanes, machine-guns, horses, or escapees from the local zoo? These sounds weren't English sounds and your mouth had to do some pretty strange things. Well, your mouth will have to do some pretty strange things now if you want it to produce an authentic foreign sound.

You're going to have to set aside your normal sense of reserve and self-consciousness and, like a child, make all sorts of strange noises. Your teacher is going to drill you in saying simple syllables over and over again: **da-da, tu-tu, oeuf-ouef, rrrr-rrrr**—until you get it. You may have to start by standing in front of the mirror, watching your mouth as you struggle to make some new sound. You are going to have to learn how to *imitate*—how to use your mouth, your throat, your entire speech mechanism, in a new way.

We take it for granted that we know our alphabet and how each letter is pronounced. But the way we pronounce the letter is *our* way, the English-speaking way, or, more accurately, the American-speaking way. There are many other ways as well, and you will need to learn the one that matches the language you are studying.

You know how it sometimes sounds when a foreigner speaks English. Even when we understand what he says it may all sound a bit "off." That's because he is using our *words,* but is making each *sound* the way he was taught to make it in his own language.

In fact, there are many different ways of pronouncing seemingly familiar sounds:

-Take the letter "t", for example. When we say the word "top", we place our tongue in a precise place against the roof of our mouth. Try it. But you can say that letter "t" slightly differently by sliding your tongue just slightly forward or back in the mouth. Sure, it sounds funny and foreign, because it's not English. But when you slide your tongue forward you are pronouncing the letter "t" more the way you might do if you spoke Spanish or French or some African languages. With your tongue more towards the back you are imitating a sound used in many languages in India.

-Or try the sound "sh" like in the word "shine". If you round your lips as you say this word, you sound like a Russian. Why? Because that is the way Russians pronounce the "sh" sound. If you try smiling as you say "shine", you are pronouncing "sh" more the way Chinese or Japanese do.

-And the letter "r" presents even greater problems. Even in England they do strange things to this sound. When "r" comes at the end of the word, like "far", most Englishmen will simply say "fah."

And if it comes at the beginning of a word, most Scotsmen will roll it. The French pronounce this sound something like a gargle in the throat that makes the word "Paris" come out something like "Paghee." So do Germans. Yet in good Chinese pronunciation the letter "r" comes out almost like an American-style "r."

What you've just learned is that foreign sounds which seem close to American English in fact are rarely the same. They are all slightly different, depending on the language. You've got to learn exactly how *your* new language makes that sound if you ever want to sound authentic.

By the way, you've just learned how to imitate a *foreign accent in English.* Actors sit down and learn how a Russian or a Chinese or an Indian pronounce various sounds of English and go from there. And they also listen a lot and imitate. So as you start learning your foreign language, remember that you are going to have to learn to be something of an *actor.* To really learn to pronounce the language well you have to ham it up a little to get into the habit of using your mouth in a whole new way. This can be fun. Just let yourself go and pretend you're starring as an exotic foreigner in a movie; you'll be on the way to getting it right.

It's a little embarrassing at first. Here you are, feeling like a child, learning to talk all over again, endlessly repeating a certain noise until the teacher thinks you're starting to get it right. But if you're in a class you are among friends. You can take your turn laughing at them, too. Once you get over the initial shock of the whole experience you'll probably find yourself enjoying the process.

For English-speakers, some languages are easier than others to learn to pronounce. Remember that few languages are *inherently* much easier or harder to pronounce than any other. It all depends on the language *you* were born with and how close the sounds of that language are to the new one you are learning.

-For English speakers, Spanish and Italian are relatively easy to pronounce because they don't have many sounds sharply different from English. But even most of these sounds are pronounced just a little bit differently than English.

-French is probably a good bit harder. French is quite fussy about the way things must be pronounced and it probably takes more effort to acquire a convincing French accent than it does a Spanish accent. (Frenchmen, too, tend to be fussier than many other nationalities about letting foreigners butcher their language.)

-Then there are languages with sounds that are rarely found in any other language—like Arabic. The Arabic language has a lot of deep guttural sounds—I couldn't possibly describe them on paper—that take a lot of work for us to get right.

-And then some African languages, such as Xhosa spoken in South Africa, have strange clicks that sound more like a wood block being struck than a human voice.

-And Chinese, Vietnamese and Thai have *tones,* or musical pitch, that help distinguish one word from another.

So be prepared for new sounds. Take them as a challenge. Don't forget to ham it up and *exaggerate.* That's the key to success in pronunciation. *Don't hang back and do the minimum with your mouth—let it all hang out and do the maximum.* That just makes it more fun—and can only contribute to your having a more authentic accent.

Another feature about foreign pronunciation: it isn't only the way each individual letter or word is spoken, but also the way it's all put together—the *intonation,* the "lilt" of the language. Mark Twain—who had a

reputation for terrible profanity—once unloaded a tor-
rent of curses in front of his long-suffering wife as he
cut himself while shaving. To teach him a lesson his
wife decided to calmly repeat each and every oath that
Twain had uttered. Unfazed at hearing this recitation,
Twain turned to his wife and said,"You've got the
words right, my dear, but you don't have the tune."

The "tune" is also important over the long run if
you want to develop a convincing accent. The into-
nations of languages differ considerably. One of the
tell-tale signs by which to recognize various languages
is the particular lilt used.

-When Americans ask a question, the intonation
in the sentence usually *rises* at the end: "Are you
going?" But an Englishman will usually *drop* his
voice at the last word when he asks the same
question. It is this intonation which is part of what
we imitate when we try to mimic the English.
Russian, Japanese, Hindi and every other language
each has its own special intonation patterns.

If this sounds hard or confusing, don't worry too
much. You can learn to speak and understand the
language without mastering these fine points. If you
ignore them too much—that is, insist on using American sound patterns instead of the patterns of your new
language—you will simply be heard to have a very
distinct American accent. If you make almost no effort
at all to learn these new patterns, however, you'll make
it very difficult for foreigners who are struggling to
understand *their* language through *your* thick American
accent.

Have you ever heard a foreigner speak English with
such a thick accent that we say "you could cut it with
a knife"? Or even worse, have you ever heard a foreigner speaking what you thought was a foreign language, only to realize a few moments later that he was
speaking English all along? That's because he was making no effort to learn the particular pronunciation of

English sounds, or English intonation patterns—even though his words were English. That's how you could sound to a foreigner if you don't make much effort to accommodate yourself to the demands of his language.

Sometimes when you are struggling to express yourself in a foreign language, you can see people straining to understand what you are saying. Watch out for this. It's a sign that you need to start putting more effort into your pronunciation. Remember, when you're overseas and off the beaten track, the people you'll meet have had little experience in understanding a foreign accent. And the less educated a person is, the less likely he is to have had much exposure to foreigners speaking his language; so the lower his tolerance will be for understanding foreign accents. Only your language teacher will be long-suffering and experienced enough to be able to understand almost anything that you say—regardless of how you butcher it.

Now I'm going to raise a point that I will be coming back to over and over again in this book. Unless you are lucky enough to be living in a foreign country already, or to have a tutor available to you for many hours a day, you are going to need a tape or cassette recorder.

Why? Because there is NO substitute for *hearing* the language—and listening and listening...and listening some more. The sounds must become completely familiar to you, so much so that you can hear them in your mind and, yes, even in your sleep.

So whenever you can, start listening to tape recordings of the lessons you are studying. Your school or language course should have them, or be able to get them. If not, be sure to ask your instructor or some native speaker to make some for you. Tapes really do make a difference.

In learning languages, *time is your friend.* The kind of sounds that you will be embarrassed or self-conscious about making in the beginning will gradually grow more familiar to you over time. Bit by bit you'll start sounding more authentic. But you have to keep working at it.

If you have a tape recorder, one useful thing you can do is to listen to yourself on the tape, especially if you can compare yourself with a native speaker. Sometimes it's discouraging because it seems that no matter how hard you try, you still have that American twang. Don't worry about it, just keep on trying. Your accent will improve with time.

You may never be able to pass for a native speaker of French, Hindi, or Japanese. That's not the point. You just want people to be able to understand you. And they *will* understand if you make a consistent effort to replace your English sounds with the sounds of their language.

KEY POINTS

1. Every language has its own way of making sounds. Some letters and sounds we think we are familiar with are pronounced slightly differently—or very differently—from English.

2. Some sounds in foreign languages will be completely new to you. Listen very carefully to the way the teacher makes the sounds. Then *imitate* and imitate and imitate.

3. *Exaggerate* the sounds when you talk. You will probably be closer to being correct than if you don't. Don't worry about feeling embarrassed. Everybody does at first. The more you ham it up, the better.

4. Get a tape recorder and practice with it all the time.

5. I'm serious. Get a recorder—and use it often.

LEARNING
LANGUAGES

CHAPTER FOUR

SWIMMING IN THE ALPHABET SOUP, OR, DON'T TRUST FAMILIAR LETTERS

In the last chapter we.talked about using your mouth in different ways. That was all about the *sounds* of a language. In this chapter we're going to talk about new ways to look at the *alphabet.*

Remember spelling bees? Does that take you back to the old days of struggling, of trying to learn to spell thousands of different words? Even after leaving school we still often have problems remembering how to spell certain words. In fact, English is an awful language to learn how to spell. Why? Because the basic spelling of English words was established hundreds of years ago and has changed only slightly since then. We are forced to write words today the way they were pronounced several centuries earlier.

-That's why we write "enough" when what we really say is "eenuf", or write "night" when we say "nite." That's why we have to go around putting on all those "silent e"s. And that's why we write "nation" when what we really say is "ney-shun." The famous British playwright George Bernard Shaw once said that logically we could spell the word "fish" as "ghoti". How? GH as in "enough", O as in "women", and TI as in "nation."

Even if that last example is a little ridiculous, it makes an important point: there is nothing especially "logical" about the way we spell in English.

Of course, you may be starting a language that uses a completely different alphabet, such as Russian, Greek, Arabic, Hindi or Korean. In one way that's almost easier, because then you don't have to learn new ways to pronounce old familiar letters. Don't ever trust familiar letters to sound like what you think they should sound like.

Dozens of foreign languages use the same alphabet as we do in English—but do so in very *different ways.* So your first task is to forget about our alphabet as we use it in English spelling and start learning how foreigners use it to represent the sounds of *their* language.

-In German and Polish, the letter "w" is always pronounced like "v". And in German the letter "v" is always pronounced like "f".

-In Latin-American Spanish, the letters "ll" are pronounced like a "y". And "j" is pronounced like "h".

-In French the letter "h" is silent.

-In English, writing the sound "sh" requires two letters—S and H—to make the one sound. In Polish the same sound is written "sz". But in

Hungarian the "sh" sound is written with the *single* letter "s". In Indonesian this sound is written as "sj". The Turks write it by inventing their own letter "s" with a hook under it. The Czechs write it by taking their own letter "s" and putting a cap over it. And in Portuguese the letter "x" is pronounced like "sh". In short, how you write the sound "sh" in this world is arbitrary.

Confusing? Yes, it can be. But remember that you will only have to learn one new set of rules in your new language—and the chances are good that your new language will spell words in a much more logical and consistent phonetic system than English. Ask any foreigner. He'll tell you that English spelling is considered just about the most difficult, inconsistent, illogical spelling system in the world.

If you're going to study Spanish the news is very good indeed. Spanish uses one of the most regular and simple spelling systems anywhere. So does Turkish. German is also quite logical. French spelling is a little bit harder, but still simpler than English.

And don't forget what we learned in the last chapter about sounds of letters. Even a "t" may be pronounced roughly as it is in English, but it may still be *slightly* different in sound. Using a pure American "t" will be understood, but it's one of those things that gives you what a foreigner will call an "American accent."

One final tip: when learning a new word, take it easy. Try sounding it out to yourself *slowly,* letter by letter, so that you can get it right. A lot of us have a tendency just to eyeball the new word and then blurt out the nearest thing that comes to mind. For instance, if we see a word like "patsa" in a foreign language, we might think we recognize it and pronounce it "pasta". But it wasn't "pasta". It was "p-a-t-s-a"—which is different. Watch out, take your time and don't let your eyes trick you. Say what's *written* and not what you think is written.

KEY POINTS

1. There is nothing "natural" at all about the way we spell English.

2. Various foreign languages use the English alphabet to write down sounds that don't sound like our sounds.

3. Be ready to pronounce familiar letters a little differently—sometimes very differently.

4. Don't leap at a guess about how a word is pronounced. Take it slowly, letter by letter.

CHAPTER FIVE

IN OTHER WORDS, LEARNING TO THINK ALL OVER AGAIN

We've talked about using your mouth in a new way. We've also described how you're likely to encounter familiar letters of the alphabet used in quite new ways. Now we're going to talk about *thinking* in a new way. This process is almost like going back to childhood once again; learning to *associate sounds with objects* the way you did when you were very young.

When you were a child, you didn't know what a tree was at first. Somebody had to tell you. Chances are your parents took you outside, pointed to a tree and said, "Tree!" I doubt that you even learned this word right away. Your parents probably had to repeat the word to you on several different occasions before you finally got the hang of it. You had to learn to associate the sound of the word "tree" with the big green leafy thing you saw in front of you.

That's what you must learn to do again. Only this time, since you're grown up, you will be able to get the hang of it much faster. You'll know why somebody is pointing to a tree, or to a picture of a tree, and saying a strange word. But you'll still have to *learn* the new word. You may even have to relearn it many times before you finally actually learn it.

There's an important idea here. Everybody in the world knows what that big green leafy thing is. We've all seen them hundreds and thousands of times. In America our name for that thing is "tree." But in Germany the name for that thing is "**Baum**." In Arab countries the name is "**shajra**." And in China they say "**shu.**" These various words are not themselves "trees". They are just some of the many hundreds of different sounds used in the world to *represent* that great big green leafy thing.

To learn a foreign language you must get away from the idea of *translating words.* Translating takes too much time and mental energy. You will never learn to really speak and understand a foreign language if you have to translate everything.

Instead, learn to *associate* the new sound directly with the image in your mind. When we hear the sound "tree" in English, we immediately associate it with that big green leafy thing. So when we hear the sound "**Baum**" or "**shajra**" or "**shu**", we don't want to think, "Hmmmm. **Baum** means tree, which means that great big green leafy thing." Doing that is translating. We want to learn to hear the sounds "**Baum**" or "**shajra**" or "**shu**" and immediately think, "Hmmm. That sound means that big green leafy thing."

You need to *establish new thought patterns by linking over and over again* a series of sounds with a mental image or an idea of an action—just as the Frenchman, Nigerian or Korean does when he hears a sound in his language which represents an object or an action. After a while the once meaningless sound becomes the new reality and image in your mind.

Don't think that the challenge of new thinking will be limited merely to the area of *new words;* it is going to go much deeper than that. You will be learning *new paths* through the woods of the mind. You can pretty well say in any other language anything that you might want to say in English. It's just that *the way of putting it* will be different—depending on the language.

Let's use a different analogy: you can build a house using materials of very different sizes and shapes. English uses one set of building blocks, but other languages will use different-shaped building blocks that take some creativity to put together at first. Where we use two blocks, they may use three smaller ones—or maybe one large one.

Here's an example of an English sentence: *We have to buy a few books before going home.* When translating into almost any foreign language you will not take *each* English word and substitute a foreign word for it. You will instead be substituting *groups of words* or *ideas* from one language to the other. How each language will choose to group the ideas depends on the language.

In French or Spanish, for example, *we have to buy* is broken down into three words: *we/have to/buy.* Why? Because *have to* is another English form of saying *must.* So we shouldn't translate each word *have* and *to* but rather the *idea of having to,* which in a large number of languages is expressed in one word—like *must.*

In Turkish, however, the Turks are able to telescope all these four words into one word, as a peculiarity of Turkish grammar. So in Turkish you would be sensitive to packaging all of those particular words into one form. We'll talk more about grammar in later chapters. To continue with our example:

-*A few* is an English idiomatic expression that in most languages is expressed in *one word.* So you learn the foreign word for *a few.*

-*Before going home* requires a little thought. In many languages like French or Russian *before going* requires three or even four words to express, given the way the grammar of those languages are. And in most languages *home* cannot be translated by one word. In this sentence *home* really means *(to) home* and many other languages will require that those *two* words be used to express it. Remember, we're not translating *words* but *ideas.*

This may seem confusing at the moment. After all, how am I to know how the other language expresses these ideas? Well, you won't know until you start to study your particular language. Each has its own time-honored peculiar way of putting things that has been worked out independently over hundreds of years or longer. Your own language course will alert you to those particular features.

-The only thing I can do for you here is to alert you to the nature of the challenge. Any given sentence in this book will be chopped apart differently when it gets translated into another language. Learn to start thinking in terms of *bundles of concepts* or *ideas* that will be converted to the new language and not *single words.*

Some of this may sound like philosophy or a complicated way to say simple things. But it really isn't. What you're trying to do is *to think* in a foreign language. Not to translate. If you don't learn to think in the foreign language, the chances are that you'll never really be very good at it.

Learning to think in a foreign language isn't all that hard. You learn to think in the language simply by using the language over and over again, asking and answering simple questions *at even the simplest level* until you feel comfortable with the process. Then you add some new words, and a few more new situations, and practice using them together with all the words you learned in previous lessons. Bit by bit you build up skill.

I don't want to suggest that you should *never* translate. There will be many times in class when the teacher will call upon you to translate a sentence that you hear or read. The point of this is to make sure that you really understand what the sentence means and that the grammar is clear to you. Sometimes when you meet an especially complicated sentence you may want to translate it to yourself, just to work it all out. But in the end you will want to go back and ensure that you can understand what it means *simply by hearing it.*

Once you really get into the language, you'll understand all this a good deal better. Somebody will be saying something quite fast and you'll suddenly realize that you understood it all! It's a great moment. Really satisfying. You probably wouldn't be able to repeat the words, or even know how it was that you understood it all. But it's a sign that the language is starting to sink into your mind. *You're beginning to understand without translating.*

In fact, serious professional translating is a very different art from speaking or understanding a language. Some people are very good at speaking, but have trouble translating well for someone else. Don't worry about this. You're trying to learn the language, not to become a translator—at least at this stage.

KEY POINTS

1. You can never really learn to speak a foreign language, or understand it when it is spoken, unless you can learn to think in the language. You can actually start to think in the language from virtually the first day.

2. Learning to think in a new language means learning to associate an initially meaningless new sound with the idea or image of what it means. You practice to the point where the new sound takes on meaning for you.

3. Avoid translating, that is, mentally putting into English everything that you read or hear. Your goal is to understand without translating.

CHAPTER SIX

LEARNING TO SPOT RELATIVES, or LANGUAGE FAMILIES

The first thing you will probably hear when you proudly announce to your friends and family that you have decided to learn Spanish, Czech, Persian, Korean, or whatever, is that the language you have chosen is "easy" or "hard." In fact, no comment about which language is easy or hard is entirely accurate.

The most important factor determining whether a language is easy or hard for you is not so much the language itself as the matter of "where you are coming from." Arabic is not very hard if you happen to speak Hebrew. Icelandic is pretty easy if you speak Danish. Russian is a cinch if you are Bulgarian.

Languages that are *close to our own* tend to be easier and more familiar, both the grammar as well as the vocabulary. But what does "close" mean? What we are actually talking about here is the matter of *language families*—an important part of understanding what languages are all about.

So let's spend a little time exploring some of the main language families of the world—and what they mean to you, in terms of learning words and grammar. You're going to end up learning lots of words in whatever new language you take up. A little understanding of language families and word associations will go a long way toward making this an easier process. It may even tell you some things about your own language, English.

All languages in the world are related to some other language or languages. And they can all be divided up into large groupings or families. Most European languages derive from a common heritage—from a very large language group or family called *Indo-European.* You may have heard of the oldest known existing written member of that language family—called Sanskrit—which was written many thousands of years ago in India.

Why does this matter to you? There's a good chance you will be learning a language from the Indo- European language family. And like all families, this one is divided into several distinct branches—like the Smiths and the Joneses who both trace their family line back to a common great-great-grandparent.

Indo-European languages subdivide into these main sub-families: Romance, Germanic, Slavic, Indic, Iranian, Celtic, and a few others such as Greek and Albanian. Let's take a slightly closer look at a few of these sub-families. Here's where you'll probably spot one of the languages that you will be studying:

Romance: (This name doesn't have anything to do with love or romantic interests, by the way. The name comes from the word Roman, simply because these languages all developed from Latin, the language of the ancient Roman Empire.) The main modern languages in this group are:

French	Spanish
Italian	Portuguese

Romanian

These languages developed when the Latin speakers of the Roman Empire became isolated in their own areas after the Empire began to fall apart. Their Latin gradually corrupted—or you could say evolved—into these various modern forms of Latin. In other words, people once speaking a common language gradually grew apart over hundreds of years until their languages began to be rather distinct one from another.

I'm giving you all this history because I want to make it clear *why* there are close relationships among all these languages. If you already know one of these Romance languages then you will find it relatively easy to learn another one of the group. The grammars are not very different and a high proportion of words will be recognizable to speakers in each of these languages. This means that with minimal work, a speaker of one can fairly quickly and comfortably learn to read another language in the same group—and with a little more work, to speak it.

You may ask, how does that help me? English isn't a Romance language. No, it isn't. It's on the next list we'll look at: the Germanic languages. I'll tell you in a moment why we English speakers can still make connections to the Romance languages.

Germanic: These languages all derived from a common Germanic ancestor, branching off from the early Indo-European prototype. The main languages in this group today are:

German	Norwegian
English	Danish
Dutch	Afrikaans (a form of Dutch)
Icelandic	Swedish

As with the Romance languages, if you know one of the Germanic languages it makes it a lot easier to learn the others. There will be big similarities in grammar and vocabulary. Some will be closer to each other than others. Languages in the same family, located geographically near one another, will generally resemble one another more than languages geographically further away. Norwegian and Swedish, for example, are much closer than are German and English.

Slavic: The oldest known written form of this family of languages is called Old Church Slavonic, a dead language now used only in the services of the Russian Orthodox Church. The main modern languages in this group today are:

Russian	Serbo-croatian (Yugoslavia)
Czech/Slovak	Polish
Bulgarian	Ukrainian (in the USSR)

Of these Slavic languages the one you're most likely to study is Russian.

I won't go into any detail about the other three large Indo-European sub-families because you're less likely to study any of them—at least as your first foreign language. The Indic languages are a large group of languages in the area of India and Pakistan. Iranian languages mainly cover Iran and Afghanistan. Celtic languages chiefly refer to Irish, Scots Gaelic and Welsh.

I promised to talk about how English fits into all of this. Well, English is actually something of an unusual language. As we've just seen, it belongs to the Germanic language family. So English *grammar* is unmistakeably Germanic in character. But the *vocabulary* of English has a lot of Romance-language words in it. When the Normans from France invaded and occupied England in 1066, they imposed thousands of French words upon the very Germanic English of that day. Even more, they imposed the basically *French system of creating new words*—the more intellectual, philosophic, cultural, scientific, and abstract words—from *Latin and Greek roots.*

As a result, our English language, starting in about the 14th century, began to reflect not only the old Germanic vocabulary but also heavy new elements of

French—which, as we saw, derived from Latin. The basically Germanic grammar of English had also grown vastly simpler. So now, the English language has a huge vocabulary—definitely more than other languages—with words from both Romance and Germanic sources. You should feel lucky that you don't have to learn English!

One advantage of having English as your native language is that you have a head start in learning either a Germanic or a Romance language. You will recognize a lot of the basic Germanic vocabulary and feel somewhat comfortable with the grammar of Germanic languages. And you'll recognize the roots of thousands of words in the Romance languages as well.

We've talked a lot of theory here. Let's now look at some concrete examples—and what these similarities mean in practice.

When you start to learn words in one of these two language families you are looking for ways to help yourself *memorize new words*. So you need to be on the look-out for words that bear some resemblance to words that are already familiar from our Romance-Germanic heritage. You can't expect to recognize every word by any means, but you should be able—with some thought and practice—to recognize many. This is a skill you want to develop.

Let's start with French. You will already know—whether you are aware of it or not—thousands of French words that are identical, or virtually identical, to English. I won't list many because they are so obviously the same, even though they might be pronounced slightly differently: **confort, assistance, question, tragédie, action, gouvernement,** etc.

There are many more French words that you would quickly recognize—at least when someone pointed out the meaning to you: **gloire, ville, heure, fleur, étrange, entière, bleu, grand, jardin, ennemi, journal** (glory, city, hour, flower, strange, entire, blue, big, garden, enemy, newspaper).

There are even more French words for which you'll need a little more imagination to relate to, or to guess. Many of these words will remind you of English words—often fancy English words from Latin roots—but the meaning will be slightly different. That's all right. You're just *looking for anything that can help you in some way to remember these words.* Try them. If you can't guess the words right off, there's nothing to worry about. What I want you to *notice is how a related English word will help you link the French word with the real English meaning in your mind.* Even if you're not going to study French you should still look at these examples to get some idea of the process of looking for related words—to serve as a memory jog in any language.

French word	English Meaning	Related English word
fort	strong	fortify
mur	wall	mural
porter	to carry	portable, porter
travailler	to work	travail
chambre	room	chamber
souvenir	to remember	souvenir shop
ami	friend	amicable
guerre	war	guerrilla
penser	to think	pensive
quitter	to leave	quit
donner	to give	donation
arrêter	to stop	arrest
rouge	red	face rouge
demander	to ask	demand
matin	morning	matinee
année	year	annual
femme	woman	feminine
lune	moon	lunar
laver	to wash	lavatory
fumer	to smoke	fumes
arbre	tree	arboretum

pont	bridge	pontoon
envoyer	to send	envoy
mort	dead	mortal, mortician
blanc	white	blank, blanch
soleil	sun	solar

I've given you quite a number of these because it's one of the most important points of all in learning a new vocabulary. You need to think about *how to relate the words you're learning to words you already know,* even if they're not exactly the same. You're looking for *handles*—memory devices—to make your memory task easier.

Now let's look at German. You remember I said the higher level terms in English come mainly from French and Latin. It's just the opposite with German. Our most basic daily words—the heart of the language—come from the Germanic origins of our language. Look at the similarity between these everyday German and English words: **Mann,** man; **Wasser,** water; **hundert,** hundred; **Haus,** house; **Apfel,** apple; **Blut,** blood.

Now look at this list for some less obvious similarities:

German word	*English Meaning*	*Related English word*
Hund	dog	hound
trinken	to drink	drink
Luft	air	aloft
rauchen	to smoke	reek
Fleisch	meat	flesh
graben	to dig	grave
schreien	to cry, shout	shriek
Licht	light	light
Morgen	morning	morning
schlafen	to sleep	sleep
Stuhl	chair	stool
Ding	thing	thing
Blume	flower	bloom

Strasse	street	street
halten	to stop	halt
vergessen	to forget	forget
lernen	to learn	learn
essen	to eat	eat

Some of the words on this German list are less like English than others. But I hope that in each case, at least after you saw the related English word—you were struck by its connection to German.

By the way, did you notice one thing? In lots of German words an "ss" comes out in English as "t" in words like **Strasse, vergessen, Wasser.** This is one of the linguistic "laws" of relationships between German and English words.

There are many such linguistic laws about how *predictable changes* come about in the way languages develop. You don't actually have to learn these laws, but some you can probably figure out for yourself, as you may have noticed in the German case above. Many of these linguistic laws are rather complex, especially when you get to languages in families more distant from English. The point is, though, that you *always need to keep your eyes open* for such connections. They may well be there. They will make your task easier.

Let's go back to the Romance languages for just one more exercise in word-association. This time let's try Spanish. Remember that Spanish, like French, comes from Latin. So the associated words that come to mind in English will also be originally from Latin—again like the French example.

Spanish word	English Meaning	Associated English word
estudiar	to study	study
sol	sun	solar
fumar	to smoke	fumes
pobre	poor	poverty
tiempo	time	tempo

vender	to sell	vending machine
recordar	to remember	record
pensar	to think	pensive
calor	heat	calorie (warms you)
tarde	late	tardy
amigo	friend	amicable
beber	to drink	beverage; imbibe
padre	father	paternal
libro	book	library
azúl	blue	azure
rojo	red	rouge
nuevo	new	new, novelty
avión	airplane	avionics
mirar	to look at	admire, mirror
cuánto	how much	quantify
levantar	to raise	levitate
escuela	school	school
seguro	sure	secure
agua	water	aquatic
palabra	word	palaver
árbol	tree	arbor
ventana	window	ventilate
enfermo	sick	infirmary

How did you do on this group of words? Are you getting the hang of it? Actually, I deliberately didn't choose many of the words that are almost exactly like English. I wanted to give you slightly harder ones to make you stretch a bit.

Did you notice a few other things? A lot of the words were similar to words we had listed in French—not surprisingly—since the languages are closely related: **arbre-árbol; penser-pensar; fumer-fumar; ami-amigo; soleil-sol; neuf-nuevo; rouge-rojo.** A lot of Spanish words began with the letter "e" that were just like an English word beginning with "s" plus consonant: **escuela, estado, estudiar.** This is another "linguistic law" in relationships between many Spanish and English words.

When you can't find obvious—or even not so obvious—connections, *look for any kind of connection. Even make one up.* We've been talking about real linguistic connections so far. But remember, you're not primarily interested in linguistic laws. You're just looking for ways to remember words. If you can develop some crazy association in your mind with a given word—that's fine.

-Let's take the Spanish word "**boleta**", which means "ticket". You may not be able to think of any word in English related to this word. But maybe the word reminds you slightly of the word ballet. (It actually has nothing to do with the word ballet.) But if you can remember the idea of "ballet-ticket" the chances are you will be able to remember that the word "**boleta**" means "ticket". After using the word a while you may not need this memory device much longer.

-One more example: the Spanish word "**ladrón**" means "thief". You might associate this word with the word "ladder". (The Spanish word "**ladrón**" actually has nothing to do with the English word "ladder" but you can remember it because thieves use ladders.)

I need to be honest with you. You'll only be able to make easy connections between English and the Romance or Germanic languages. When we look at words from other sub-families of the Indo-European group the process of making connections gets much harder. It takes a lot more knowledge of linguistic rules to spot *any* connections if you are studying Russian, any other Slavic language, or one of the Indian languages. That's one reason why those languages are considered harder for us than Romance or Germanic languages.

So the more remote the language you're learning is from English, the more you'll need to use your imagination to make connections. Otherwise it will be very difficult to memorize and use thousands of words that you can't get a "memory handle" on.

The whole point of imagination is that you *have to make the connections in your own mind* if your memory tricks are going to work. This is true even if the connections are totally phony, or even wild. Let me give you a few more examples of how I, at least, might go about trying to remember a number of Russian words that have no obvious connections with their English equivalents—by making "phony connections."

> **derevo** means "tree": reminds me of "derive" alcohol from wood.
> **tratit'** means "spend": reminds me of "treating" a friend.
> **yazyk** means "language": vaguely like "music" of language.
> **nebo** means "sky": a "nebbish" has his head in the clouds.

Look, I know I'm really stretching a point here. Some of these word associations I made up are almost absurd. But they do serve to give me a way, however tortured, to remember the word the first few times I see it in a word list. A word that was meaningless and looked like gibberish suddenly takes on personality and character. That's what remembering a word is all about. *You can throw away the word association crutch once the word has become real to you* and begun to sink into your memory. So go ahead and dream up your own "connections" to help you remember. What works is right for you.

Of course, the more languages you learn the easier this process becomes. First of all, you just get more experienced at making up your own memory devices day after day. Second, the more languages you know, the more words you know that remind you of something else. You get much faster at "spotting handles."

Non-Indo-European languages:

Many of you will be studying languages that are not part of the Indo-European family. These languages will present even greater difficulty since there is no reason whatsoever for words in these languages to have any connection with English. Still, even here you'll find many words borrowed in more recent times from English.

All is not hopeless however, especially if you are going to be learning more than one language from a given area. In the Middle East, for example, there are also a number of language families. Should you ever become serious about studying more than one language of this region, your job will be relatively easy if your second language belongs to the same family as your first.

-For example, Hebrew and Arabic are very closely related. If you know one language it's fairly easy to spot word relationships in the other, and the grammar is fairly similar.

-Moreover, Arab/Islamic culture spread all over the Middle East, North Africa, and much of south and south-east Asia in the Middle Ages. So even though most of the languages in the area are *not* in the same family at all as Arabic, the regional languages absorbed great quantities of Arabic words.

Most of these Arabic loan words were adopted to express new Islamic terms relating to cultural, literary, scientific or philosophical concepts in the fields of history, law, literature, religion, and economics. These Arabic terms are generally identical in languages unrelated to Arabic—languages like Turkish, Persian, Urdu (Pakistan), Hindustani, Malaysian, Indonesian, and Swahili (in much of Africa)—wherever Islam spread. So here again, just as Latin is the basis of much of the educated concepts of Western languages, Arabic plays the same role in the Muslim world.

Turkish is related to a very large family of Turkic languages that are spoken across a huge geographic belt from Turkey east through northern Iran, Soviet Central Asia and Western China. They may be exotic languages you're not too likely to learn—Uzbek, Kazakh, Turkmen, Azerbaijani, Uighur, etc., but once you learn Turkish you've taken a huge step forward towards learning the virtual *lingua franca* or common language of an area covering several thousand miles, from the borders of Greece to the borders of Mongolia.

East Asian languages are even more elusive to the English speaker. Japanese and Chinese words seem to lack the separate and distinctive sounds of English or other Western languages. From some points of view they might be considered harder to learn. Chinese (Thai and Vietnamese, too) uses tones to distinguish among different words. So a word in Mandarin Chinese like **"yan"** could mean either tobacco, color, eye, or test, (or more) depending on the tone (high, rising, falling, low) that the particular word has. That complicates learning vocabulary if you don't happen to have a good ear and memory for tones. The only consolation is that Chinese grammar is very easy.

Now you have some sense of what experts are talking about when they say that this or that language is related. When the language you are learning is related to one you already know, your task is easier. You can also begin to understand why people who have already learned a number of languages generally find it reasonably easy to go on and learn several more. It always involves work. But it becomes easier when you have experience and "friends" among several different language "families."

KEY POINTS

1. All languages belong to language families. If the language you are studying comes from a nearby family

such as the Romance or Germanic language group, look for similarities. They are there.

2. Even if you can't always spot similarities (they're not always there), use your imagination to try to make up connections in your own mind to help you remember the word. Later you can drop the memory device.

3. In languages distant from or totally unrelated to English, you will have to rely even more on your imagination and memory tricks to remember many thousands of words that have no relationship to English.

4. The more languages you learn, the better you get at spotting real, or inventing artificial, connections in your mind to help you remember.

5. Anything that helps you remember a word is fair game.

CHAPTER SEVEN

DIGGING UP WORDS BY THEIR ROOTS

W e spent a good bit of time in the last chapter talking about language families and the kinds of similarities to look for among them. We also talked about the use of imagination to help you make connections between English words and their foreign counterparts.

In this chapter I want to show you another fundamental fact about languages that will greatly simplify your memory task. It is this: every language builds its *complex* words from the simple basic word roots of that language. This means the difficulty of learning strange and unrelated words will come mainly at the *beginning,* when everything is new to you. But as you begin to get hundreds, or even a thousand, words under your belt you will start noticing that an increasing proportion of the subsequent new words you learn are based on the roots of the basic words you have already learned.

When you think about it, this makes sense. Primitive human beings painstakingly and gradually created new sounds, new words, as the need arose. They needed

clearly distinguishable words for every new object—
basic things like "fire, water, wood, food," and so forth.
But as people needed to expand their language and
create more sophisticated concepts they drew on many
of the existing roots of the language as their basis for
creating new words. Every language does this. As these
new words were created, each language developed certain rough *patterns* for the creation of new vocabulary.
In other words, each language has its own distinctive
characteristics for generating new words.

*Your job is to figure out how the language you're
studying actually works, and how it generates its new
words.* You won't have to analyze the pattern on your
own—your teacher and your text can help you to do
that. You need only be aware that there *is* a system
and pattern your language uses to "invent" new words.
It's an irregular and not fully predictable pattern—but
it's a pattern.

To help you get the idea, let's take a look at how
we do it in English. In English we can sometimes make
up new words from basic Germanic roots largely by
putting simple endings on them.

- From the adjective "dark" we create the verb
"darken."
- From the adjective "quick" we create the verb
"quicken."
- From the adjective "bright" we create the verb
"brighten."
- From the noun "strength" we create the verb
"strengthen."

Get the pattern? You can see that English has a
system—they never teach it in school—that let's you
make verbs out of *some* words by adding "-en". So if
you were an Indonesian learning English you might
have to struggle to learn the word "bright" the first
time you saw it. But you would be very quick to learn
the verb "brighten" once you had learned "bright." On
the other hand, the pattern doesn't always work. We

can't say "smallen" from "small" or "greenen" from
"green", even if we can say "redden" from "red". Languages develop from human social usage, not from
computers or mathematicians or professors.

We also have thousands of words that are combi-
nations of root words: book-bag, doorknob, icebreaker,
fishburger, windbreaker, eyewash, dogfood, candle-
stick. Or words extending from simpler roots such as
life: lively, living, liven, live, lifeless.

These are simple examples of word-building which
English has retained from the old Germanic system.
But most of our word building comes from using the
French/Latin system. For example, we use the old An-
glo-Saxon "write" in our every day language about
writing: write, writer, re-write, writings, etc. But when
we want to create more complex, abstract words related
to the idea of "writing" we turn to the Latin root
"scribe"—which is just the everyday Latin root for
"write." And we add *Latin* prefixes. So we end up with
a whole series of different words for more complex
concepts that come from the simple idea of writing:

inscribe which means literally to "write into."
describe which means literally to "write about."
subscribe which means literally to "write under"
or "sign up to", or "underwrite" in the sense that
"I subscribe to that idea."
prescribe which means literally to "write first" or
"write in the beginning" in the sense of writing
authoritatively, such as a medicine is "prescribed"
to a patient.
proscribe which means literally "write forward",
publicize it, or forbid it.
transcribe which means literally "write across",
from one system to another, such as transcribe
shorthand notes into regular writing.
conscribe which means literally "write together
with", such as writing names with other names on
a list for conscription.

ascribe which means literally "write to" or "write toward", such as ascribing a certain characteristic to someone.

In German, or Russian, or most other languages, this process is less mystifying, because it's more self-contained. They use their *own* everyday word for "write" and add on their *own* prefixes to create roughly the same abstract words like "subscribe, transcribe, prescribe" etc., unlike our use of *foreign* roots and *foreign* prefixes.

-So in German, using the word **schreiben**—to write, we get
zuschreiben—to ascribe; **zu**=to
einschreiben—to register; **ein**=in
vorschreiben—to prescribe; **vor**=first, before
ausschreiben—to advertise, write out; **aus**=out
aufschreiben—to write down; **auf**=on, onto
umschreiben—to transcribe; **um**=around, about
beschreiben—to describe; **be**=to cause

By the way, did you happen to notice the similarity between "scribe" in Latin and "**schreiben**" in German? It's not by accident. Both are Indo-European languages and happen to share this root word.

In Russian, using the regular Russian word **pisat'**—to write, we get:
opisat'—to describe; **o**=about
perepisat'—rewrite; **pere**=over
podpisat'—to subscribe; **pod**=under
pripisat'—to ascribe; **pri**=to
nadpisat'—to inscribe; **nad**=above, over
vypisat'—to write out, prescribe; **vy**=out
zapisat'—to write down, register; **za**=down

Now you can see how words are built up. Once you learn the basic word, you can spot how the more complex words are created from it. Of course, you still have to study the word to learn it. No system is fully predictable and each has lots of irregularities. But the learning process becomes much easier when you have something to hang your memory on. And most Indo-European languages employ this system of *combining basic roots and prefixes* to create more complex concepts.

Let's remember that English is a living language. The meanings of a lot of our words have evolved over time. So they don't all have quite the same literal meaning that they started out with. A word like "manufacture" literally means "hand-made": *manu*—hand and, *facture*—made; because in the old days when you manufactured something you made it by hand. But you can see that the basic principle of the word is still there. And a knowledge of how to dissect these words will help you learn them—especially if you were starting to learn English as a foreign language.

The point is that words are not just a *complicated set of meaningless syllables* that have a certain arbitrary meaning attached to them. A language *grows*, organically, like a tree. So it's natural for words to be related to one other and built from each other. We don't make up some meaningless new sound and give it a meaning. We almost always work from existing words to create new ones.

If an American or British scientist invents some kind of new machine, you can bet that he won't decide to call it a *gropsmaflupyim*. Why? Because that's not English, nor does it even look like English. Just because he invented it doesn't really give him the right to make up a name out of the blue. Why not? He's breaking the rule that you make up new words out of existing roots of the language. Furthermore, nobody would ever remember the name. It would hardly be on the road to commercial success. But if he called it a *transtactomorpholator*, you'd immediately accept it as English, even though I just made the word up out of Latin and Greek roots used in English.

Remember: every language will have some sort of word-building system. Look for it. After all, if there weren't some kind of a system, kids wouldn't be able to learn their own language either.

KEY POINTS

1. Every language builds the complex words from the simple basic root words of that language.

2. After you learn several hundred words or more you will start noticing familiar roots creeping back into your vocabulary lists in new forms.

3. Eventually, the vast proportion of new vocabulary in your new language will be based on roots you already know.

CHAPTER EIGHT

"WORDS, WORDS, WORDS..."
(Shakespeare, Hamlet)

There are only two things that you really need to learn when you study a foreign language: words, and how to put them together. (All right, so all you need to build the Eiffel Tower is some bolts and girders and a lot of space! Fair enough.) You just can't learn a language without learning words—lots of them. Memorizing vocabulary lists—and grammar rules, which determine how you use these words—can be the real drudgery of language study. I want to show you how to make learning vocabulary as easy and painless as possible.

How many words do you have to learn when you study a language? Well, that depends on what you want to say—and understand. To get around a country and meet your very basic needs, a couple of hundred words might do. To carry on a simple conversation on general topics you'll need about two thousand words. To hold a fairly serious conversation with people and to read a newspaper you'll need a minimum of five thousand words. Don't worry about the numbers now. At any stage the most important thing is to *use all the words you know.*

The traditional way to study vocabulary is to use a word list, with the foreign words listed down one side and the corresponding English words down the other. You cover up one side of the page and go down the other while practicing and testing yourself until you think you know them all pretty well.

The main problem with a list is that you can cheat a little bit. You sometimes remember what a word on a list means, not because you actually remember the word, but because you remembered which word came after which on the list. Or you remember which word it was that came near the top of the list. Put the word in a different place on the list and suddenly you don't remember what it means any more.

Instead of lists, I recommend you use *word cards* to learn vocabulary. Word cards are a variation on the idea of word lists but they don't have the drawbacks of lists. In fact, word cards have many extra advantages.

First let me describe word cards. They are little cards—the thickness of index cards—about 1" x 3" with the foreign word written on one side and the English on the back. Don't buy the ready-made ones with the preprinted vocabulary on them—they're expensive and half the time they don't have the words on them that you want, or the way you want them. Buy blank cards and write your own. When you make your cards, write the word upside down on the second side, so that you have only to flip the card upside down to see the meaning. If you can't find boxes of blank word cards for sale, make your own by cutting up index cards.

The advantages of word cards as a technique for collecting and drilling vocabulary are:

-You can mix the order of the cards around, which means you won't remember the meaning of the card just from its place on the list.

-As you go through the vocabulary cards of a new lesson you will learn some words very quickly. These you can weed out, keeping in the pile only the words that you haven't mastered. This permits you to concentrate your effort on the smaller number of harder words.

-You can keep together those words from all the lessons that are your particular bugbear—the ones you just can't seem to remember. (This will be a pile to pick up often.)

-You can always grab a little stack of cards (with a rubber band around them) and take them with you somewhere if you think you may have to while away some time on the bus, or in a dentist's waiting room, or wherever.

There are three steps to memorizing vocabulary:

—Find memory handles.
—Say the words out loud.
—Go for speed.

Find memory handles. Just as with anything else, there are techniques to memorizing words that can make the process easier. We spent a lot of time in previous chapters talking about how to make word associations. You may notice a similarity with an English word—just as we discussed in our chapter on language families. You may notice a similarity with some word you have already learned in your new language—as we talked about in our chapter on word roots. Or the word may remind you of something— possibly unrelated—which helps let the word stick in your mind. However you do it, get a handle on the word.

Say the words out loud. As you go through your word cards always say each word out loud, or at least whisper it to yourself. Remember, you are training several parts of your head at once: your *mind* (by thinking about the whole process), your *eye* (by seeing and recognizing the word), your *mouth* (by saying the word as you study it), and your *ear* (by hearing what you are saying to yourself). Saying the word and hearing it are as important as seeing it. And use your best hammed-up foreign pronounciation. You may feel self-conscious at first about talking to yourself, but you'll soon get over that. Language study can pretty quickly hammer the shyness out of you.

Go for speed. Go over the word list or the pile of word cards until you can run through them fast. It isn't really good enough if you have to puzzle over each word before you remember the meaning. Remember that you are trying to reach the stage where you *don't have to think*—you want to get to the point where you can almost go *automatically* from the foreign word to English. This is not an intellectual exercise. You are learning to *build automatic language reflexes* through repetition.

Always start with the foreign language side of the word card face up first. This is actually the easier part of the learning process. All you have to do is to remember what the foreign word means. Here's where your memory tricks are most important. They help you recognize the foreign word and learn its meaning. You don't really need the memory trick any more after you start recognizing the word. You want to get where you don't have to think about it any more.

After you have the foreign words down fairly cold, turn the cards over and start going from the English word *back* to the foreign word. This is usually harder. Now you have to remember *precisely* what the foreign word is. But at least you'd already seen it and said it several times when you were looking at it earlier and trying to remember the English.

Always do the cards *both ways,* first the foreign language to English and then English to the foreign language. Just going one way is not good enough. For some reason the mind sees these as different processes. Doing it one way is no guarantee that you can do it the other. Going from the foreign language to English is passive: you just want to see how fast the meaning can sink into your mind. Going from English to the foreign language is an *active* process where you are training your mind to think in a foreign language.

Don't use the cards exclusively for single words. You should also make up cards with phrases or expressions that you especially want to learn. And by all means put additional information on the card about words that you need to remember, such as special forms or irregularities or whatever.

As you learn the words, it really helps to try to make up sentences out of the new words. This makes the new words more real. And, at the same time, you'll be able to use other words that you've already learned. You will be reinforcing sentence structures as well.

Every so often, go back and review the words you learned earlier. You may find you have forgotten some of the ones you haven't used very often. You may also find you can flip through those old cards a lot faster than you ever were able to do before. That's a sure sign that you're making progress—even when you thought you weren't.

Remember, making these word cards and studying them is all part of the process of repetition—an essential part of the language process. You're trying to implant a whole new language into your mind. Rome wasn't built in a day. Neither were Paris or Madrid or Tokyo or Moscow either.

KEY POINTS

1. Home-made word cards are an excellent technique for memorizing vocabulary.

2. Use those memory handles to fix the meaning of the new vocabulary in your mind.

3. Learn words first from the foreign language to English, and then the other way. Learning them one way does not mean you know them well the other way.

4. Always say the foreign word out loud as you see it—don't just read it. You want to involve your mouth and your ears as well as your eyes.

5. Don't be passive. Make up little sentences to yourself using the new word. Do the maximum with the new vocabulary, not the minimum.

CHAPTER NINE

STRINGING WORDS TOGETHER

For the first few lessons your text may not dwell much at all on grammar. These days dialogues are a popular way to start to learn a language. You learn a simple dialogue—usually representing an American (you) talking to a real live foreigner just after you have arrived in his country. But when you memorize these dialogues you *are* learning grammar without being aware of it. The foreign grammar patterns are being unconsciously imprinted in your mind.

Once you have some of these "canned sentences" memorized so that you can say them in your sleep, you can easily substitute some of the other new vocabulary to make new sentences. "Where is the *station?*" (airport, bus stop, hotel, taxi stand).

The dialogues at this early stage should be useful and simple—the kinds of conversations you are likely to get into often. Don't be disappointed by the things that you will be talking about at this stage of your lessons. It's going to be limited mostly to talking about your name, how you are, where you're from and how to get to the airport. You'll have to wait till later to get into conversations about philosophical topics, whether the governmental coalition is beginning to crumble, or how the trade imbalance is likely to affect the national inflation. First things first...

At this early stage of your language study you should also be ready to learn lots of polite phrases. Foreigners like polite phrases. They generally use them more than we do in English. Better than that, these kinds of polite phrases are great "fillers" which you can throw in whenever you can't think of anything else to say. Or you can stick them into your conversations and sound like you know more than you do.

Remember, at the beginning you won't likely be making up too many of your own sentences. This is the small talk stage: welcome, how are you, I am fine, how is your family, how do you like Japan, are you an American, how long have you been in Paris, have you been to a bullfight, how much do the egg rolls cost, and so on.

This material will be very important to you. It is the first stage of your becoming the actor I told you about. You should take to repeating these dialogues as if your Academy Award depended upon it. It can actually be fun trying to play the foreigner in the way that I talked about earlier. You want to try to exaggerate all the new sounds and take on your new foreign personality. *But the real point of this drill is to drive these dialogues into your memory until they have become second nature. You want to be able to repeat these patterns of conversation without even having to think.*

After you have repeated these sentence patterns many times—most usefully with another person—you will already have begun to think in the language. OK, you won't be thinking profound thoughts. Don't rush off to the Presidential Palace or the University to try out your new skills yet. That will come later. But you are asking questions and giving appropriate answers in a foreign language. *You are already starting to think in the language.*

How well do you have to know a language to start dreaming in it? One year, two years, almost a lifetime? Wrong. You can actually start dreaming in a language in a few weeks. Whether you do or not partly depends on you and your tape recorder, or the amount of hours you spend each day on language study. If you really listen a lot, and repeat and repeat your sentences, you'll soon find them swimming around in your head. When you go to sleep at night you'll find yourself repeating them over and over—even in your sleep. That's a great sign. It's a sign the language is really getting to you—and into you.

You don't have to know a lot of the language to start using it. To some extent this is going to depend on the textbook you are using and your teacher's own method of teaching. The main thing is that whatever sentences you find in the first few lessons of your book, you and your teacher should be able to form conversational questions from them. If your book has a dialogue about "where is the airport", you can start asking—and answering—where the airport is. Never mind that this is just a "canned dialogue" straight out of the book. The point is that you are *hearing* a question in the language, *understanding* it, and *answering* it. That is what thinking in the language is all about.

You want to "exercise" the material as often as you can. That is, you want to practice the new words by using them in sentence patterns you already know. Here are some examples of what we mean by "exercising":

-Where is the pencil?
-Is the pencil on the table? (Give yes and no full
    sentence answers)
-What is on the table?
-Where is the book?
-Is the pencil on the book?
-My name is John.
-Are you John?
-Is he John?

-Where is John?
-Is John an American?
-What is his name?
-Is his name John?
-Am I John?
-Is he American?
-Is the book American?
-Where is John?
-Is John on the table?

This may seem simple-minded. It isn't. You are *already* speaking a foreign languge. With each chapter you will learn new words which you can exercise and mix back into the old sentences. You're getting more comfortable with the whole process of hearing, understanding and now *generating* your own sentences.

Using a Tape Recorder

Now I'm going to bring up the old business about the tape recorder again. Get hold of a tape recorder and some tapes. You need to listen, and listen, and listen to the material.

Here's how to use your tapes. First, listen to the lesson several times until you think you can generally follow what it says.

Next, listen to each sentence and then put the recorder on "pause" and repeat out loud the sentence you just heard (Some tapes already have pauses built into the recording, giving you enough time to repeat the sentence). If you have trouble saying it all, then listen to the same sentence again and try repeating it again.

Go through the tape out loud several times until you are really pretty comfortable at doing this. I know you may feel self-conscious, or view it as something more suited to a ten-year-old. But believe me, it works. The reason it works is that when you listen to the tape you are training your ear. Your mind is beginning to understand the foreign words without taking out time to translate them.

I just can't emphasize enough how important it is to listen and repeat with a tape recorder. No other technique can get you to understand and speak the language as fast as this one.

If you can't get any tape recordings at all then try to find somebody who can record your lessons or dialogues for you on a blank tape. At the absolute worst, you can record the material yourself. That won't do much for your accent—since your accent is likely to be rather American at the start—but it is still much better than nothing. At least you will be listening, understanding and repeating/speaking—the most important exercises of all.

KEY POINTS

1. You can start using the language right away by learning and using the dialogues in your book.

2. Use a tape recorder to listen to the dialogues or the sentences and repeat them, until you can do so comfortably. This process is one of the most valuable things you can do to learn a foreign language.

3. Memorizing whole sentences helps teach you the patterns of the language and imprints them on your mind.

CHAPTER TEN

GRAMMAR (UGH)

Can grammar be fun? Well, almost... At least interesting.

We all remember sitting through tedious sessions of English grammar in school. It seemed almost impossible for that to be interesting, right? But learning the grammar of a foreign language is different. The grammar is really the skeleton of the language. A language, after all, consists of basically two things.

-One is words—the flesh and clothing of the language.

-The other is grammar—the bones of the language, which hold it all together.

You never really needed to study English grammar to learn how to talk. You already knew the grammar when you started talking. But how did you learn grammar? Not out of any book, that's for sure. And your parents probably never really taught you much actual grammar, either. You learned grammar by *hearing it used* all around you all day long.

Let's talk a little bit about how small children learn their own language. It's important because it tells us something about how every one of us learned our first language. That will give you a few ideas about how to to go about learning a foreign language.

There are great debates among language specialists about how children learn a language. For a while a lot of experts thought that children spoke only by repeating specific things that they had heard. This theory suggested, in effect, that kids learn to speak by being little tape recorders. In theory they would hear a phrase, and then at some later time they would spew that same sentence forth again under different circumstances.

But if you think about it for one minute—or if you have ever spent much time around your own child or a little brother or sister—you would know that this theory is not quite right. Even a child of two knows some grammar rules—unconsciously. Have you ever heard a young child say something like, "I *singed* a song."? Has he ever heard anyone utter such a phrase? No, never, simply because no native speaker of English over five years old would ever say such a thing.

Then why did the child say it? Because he had already heard enough sentences in his short life to have figured out a few grammar rules on his own. He figured out that if you are using the past tense—the term we use in grammar to describe something that has already happened—that you put a "-ed" on the end of the word. What that child had not been around long enough to know was that some verbs are "irregular", that is, they don't quite follow the rules. The child had heard sentences like "I walked the dog", or "I slammed the door", or "It rained a lot yesterday", so he assumed you would do the same thing with "I singed a song."

Another example: A young child might say, "My cat caught three mouses." Now, that child has never heard anyone say "mouses." But he has absorbed the grammar rule that when you've got more than one of something you put an "-s" on the end. So he's applying a rule that nobody ever told him about.

Actually, the way a child learns his first language is a fairly good method. In fact, if you're a small child, there is probably no better way to learn a language than that way. And it's virtually painless. But alas, it's not so practical for us to learn a language that way now.

Why not? First of all, it takes about four or five years of around-the-clock study for a child to learn to speak the grammar correctly. You don't have time for this type of total immersion learning. We've all got much better things to do with our time. Second, for an adult, it is rather a pain to learn a language by listening to thousands upon thousands of sentences and then trying to figure out the grammar rules by example. There must be easier ways.

There are. As grown-ups, we can take advantage of our brains and our power of logic. We can learn the grammar in a more organized way than the child does. For example, after hearing one or two examples of sentences in a foreign language someone can tell us, "OK, when you have a sentence like this in the present tense and you want to make it past tense, all you do is ...." (depending on the language).

Let's go back to the old tape recorder again. I've already mentioned that you should never leave home without it. You should spend a lot of time listening to tapes and memorizing sentences and phrases.

Now you should see why tape recorders are so important. *Listening to the tape recorder is the adult equivalent (only in a less haphazard way) of being the child and listening to adults chattering around you all day long.* It puts patterns of language into your head in an organized way so that they become second nature. When these patterns have become etched in your mind, you can learn how to play around with them, to make variations on the patterns.

If you ever had to learn a foreign language "the old-fashioned way," you might recall that you had to learn long lists of verb endings—as mere rules and without any conversational drill. (A screaming bore and not necessarily all that useful.) An up-to-date language course will let you learn a few hunks of pattern sentences at a time—learning them cold. Then you can learn something about the grammatical rules. These rules let you "manipulate" the grammar (a word linguists love to use—it just means play around with the grammar to change the meaning of the words you have learned.)

Learning the grammar is a bit like driving a car or learning how to use any other complex machine. It might be fine for you to know how to steer a car down the road in third gear if somebody shows you how. But nobody can really consider that he knows how to drive a car until he has learned to "manipulate" all parts of the car. You will want to know how to use the brakes and the other gears and a lot of other important things before you really feel comfortable in the car.

It's the same with a language. You can learn a lot of words and sentences, but until you know how to use these words in lots of different ways and change them all around, you can't really consider that you know the language very well. You don't really know how to "drive" the language yet.

We all tend to think of grammar as meaning how to speak "correctly." But grammar rules are *not* basically designed to make people speak correctly. They are designed to help people *get their meaning across* accurately and clearly. They are meant to be shortcuts, or operating rules, that help you put together the words. They save you the hassle of having to painfully decide for yourself how you make a word plural or how to say that you "did" something instead of "are doing" something.

If a foreigner were learning English, for example, he would have to learn how to use various forms of the English verb. He would study sentences like "I *go* to London. I *went* to London. *Did* you *go* to London? *He would have gone* to London. *Were* they *going* to London? When *will* she go to London? You *have gone* to London." Believe me, after you get done with that type of practicing you are positively carsick. But you will have learned a lot about the verb "to go" and how to use it.

The fact is that a huge list of words is not much good *if you don't know how all the words go together.* You might be able to blurt out enough words in some crude way that will get across your basic needs. But your goal here is not to sound like a caveman—"Me go London." "Give food." You hope actually to be able to talk like a reasonably educated person. That means knowing how the words go together—or what we call the grammar.

When you learn the grammar you are getting "inside" the language. You are starting to figure out how people of that country actually use their mental processes to express themselves. The grammar is really the key to this new world you are entering. It describes the set of building blocks that is unique in every language. It is the "secret code"—the concepts in which Frenchmen or Russians or Arabs or Burmese think.

Pay close attention to this part of the process. You will be surprised—maybe fascinated—at the *distinctions* that other languages take great care to spell out, which in English *we* don't care so much about. Or at the distinctions in English which we seem to care about expressing but which another language doesn't. Let me give you some examples:

Speakers of Russian, French, Turkish and many other languages *change the endings of the verb* to indicate whether it is "I" who am talking about myself (so-called "first person"), or if I am addressing "you" ("second person"), or if I am talking about some third person—"he" or "she." So a Russian would use these endings in a verb in the present tense:

1st	I know	Ya znay**u**
2nd	You (one person) know	Ty znay**esh**
3rd	He (or she or it) knows	On znay**et**
1st pl.	We know	My znay**em**
2nd pl.	You (several people) know	Vy znay**ete**

3rd pl.   They know   Oni znayut

A Turk would do it this way:

1st	I know	biliyorum
2nd	You know	biliyorsun
3rd	He, she, it knows	biliyor
1st pl.	We know	biliyoruz
2nd pl.	You (plural) know	biliyorsunuz
3rd pl.	They know	biliyorlar

But if you use the word "I","you", or "he", what need is there to have to put an extra "ending" on the end of the verb? Good question. In English we don't do it that way any more. (Old English did.) But in Russian, or Turkish, you *have to do it that way* because that's the way the language works. The ending on the verb *has to indicate who it is that is talking.* If you put the wrong ending on the verb you will completely confuse your listener because the wrong ending might mean "I vomit" instead of "you vomit"—a distinction in which you might have an interest. (And the verbs in a great number of other languages you're likely to study work that way too.)

But hold on. Even in English we did make one change. We suddenly put an "-s" on the end of the "he" form. We can say "I know, you know", but "he know*s*". Why? Because that's the way English works. The third person form always has to have an "-s" ending. Furthermore, it's not correct without it. Sure, you could understand it without the "-s" on the end— "he go". But that's not the way the language works. And it sounds like Tarzan.

Actually there is a reason why most languages— even Old English—put endings on verbs to denote "person". The point was that the actual verb—without the pronouns "I", "you", or "he" or whatever—could be used by *itself.* In Russian today you can use just the one word "znayete" and it's clear that you mean "you know" without actually using a second word "vy" meaning "you". Before dismissing verb endings as "un-English" and impossible to master, take a look at Shakespeare or even at the Bible. You'll find lots of phrases like "thou knowest" and "whither goeth John." These don't give us a problem there, so we shouldn't be bothered by verb endings in foreign languages. Our own language simplified itself many hundreds of years ago so it doesn't draw those distinctions anymore, except in the "he" "she" "it" form where it keeps the ancient "-s" ending.

But then from the point of view of some other languages, English is fussy where they are not: In Chinese they say "one book, two book, many book", while in English we have to put an "-s" on the end of each word to show it is plural: "one book", but "two books, many books". The Chinese asks, "Why do you need to put an "-s" on the end of the word when the words "two" and "many" already clearly indicate that there is more than one book anyway?" The Chinese would be right—from his point of view. But you have to remember that languages are never intrinsically logical. And each speaker of a language thinks the way that *other people* speak their language is illogical, complicated or unnecessary.

Both Arabic and Hebrew have different words for "you" (to a man), and "you" (to a woman), in addition to a difference in verb ending. An English speaker would say, "That's completely unnecessary. One word "you" does perfectly well for both." Who's right?

The Turks have just *one* word for "he", "she", and "it". They look at English and say, "Why do you have three different words for these things when one word does perfectly well for all of them?". Japanese and Javanese (Indonesia) regularly distinguish between levels of politeness by the verb they use.

The fact is, you can't really spend time arguing about such matters. That's just the way they are. But it is interesting to see how thought processes differ from language to language—and country to country. That's what languages are all about. And that's why language study teaches us so much about foreign cultures, and about our own language as well. Things that we take for granted as "natural" turn out not to be natural at all, but simply the way that we do things.

KEY POINTS

1. Grammar is the skeletal structure that links words together and gives them full meaning.

2. Correct grammar is not so much designed to create elegant speech as it is to make clear what the relationship is among words. This is why we have to learn it.

3. Each language makes its own sharp distinctions. You need to be ready to: a) learn new distinctions that we don't make in English, and b) ignore the distinctions we make in English that are not there in the foreign language.

CHAPTER ELEVEN

NO END TO ENDINGS (MORE UGH)

In the last chapter we talked about what grammar is, and how—even as small children—we can know it without having to study it. We saw that each person feels his own language says things the "natural" way. We also talked a little about word endings—especially on verbs. In this chapter we're going to take a longer look at endings: specifically at how some languages put different endings on *nouns*.

One key difference between English and many other languages is that some others fuss a lot with the ends of nouns. In English, whether you've ever realized it or not, we rely largely on *word order* to convey meaning. "The dog bites the cat" and "The cat bites the dog" have very different meanings. So what? Everyone knows that if you change the word order you change the meaning.

But for a lot of other languages this simply isn't so. They depend largely on *endings* on the words to make the meaning clear. In Russian, for example, it is quite possible to reverse the order of "dog bites cat" to "cat bites dog" and still mean exactly the same thing: the cat got bitten. Why? Because in Russian the word order isn't all that important. In Russian you have to put an *ending* on the nouns to indicate which is the *subject* and which is the *object,* that is, who is the "biter", and who is the "bitee".

How? In Russian a large body of nouns end in "-a" when the word is the subject (or "biter") of the sentence. That same noun changes its ending to "-u" when it becomes the object of the sentence (or the "bitee"). So the word "koshka" (cat) becomes "koshku" when it moves from "biter" to "bitee". In the same way "sobaka" (dog) becomes "sobaku" when it becomes the one that gets bitten. So in Russian it really doesn't make much difference exactly what the word order is, the meaning is still the same. In Russian, **Sobaka ku-sayet koshku** and **Koshku kusayet sobaka** both mean "The dog bites the cat." But in English word order makes the crucial difference about who gets bitten.

Of course, not all of you will be studying languages in which the word order is as unimportant as it is in Russian. But many languages in the world behave in the same way, preferring to use signals or codes, or endings—or whatever you want to call them—at the end of words to signal to you about who is doing what to whom. Other languages which do this to some extent or another include German, Latin, Greek, nearly all the Slavic languages (Polish, Czech, Serbian, etc.) Turkish, Persian and hundreds of other more obscure ones.

English, French and Spanish, have almost totally dropped these endings on nouns yet still cling on to them when it comes to pronouns—those little words that "stand in" for nouns. In English we make a distinction between most subject and object pronouns:

Subject Pronouns: I you he she it we they

Object Pronouns: me you him her it us them

Boy chases girl.

He chases her.

We don't say "He chases she."

We've just talked about one kind of ending here, the ending used to denote the *subject* of the sentence as opposed to the direct *object*. But many languages have more than just that one kind of ending, or "case". Another very common case is called the *genitive* case, or more commonly in English grammar, the *possessive* case. As you might guess, it is the ending that denotes possession.

We have an ending to denote possession in English, just as do most of the Germanic languages, Slavic languages, and many others in the Indo-European family (but not the Romance languages for some reason). In English the ending is "-'s" (apostrophe s). "The dog's bone" means "the bone of the dog." In fact, "the bone of the dog" is the *only* way you can express it in Romance languages like French or Spanish. Many other languages that use the possessive case, however, prefer to put it the other way around, by saying "the bone dog's" which means, "the bone of the dog."

In still other languages, endings tacked onto nouns take the place of separate English prepositions, such as "to" "from" and "at". Turkish nouns provide a good example. Every noun in Turkish can have the following case endings attached to it.

ev= house
evin= of the house
eve= to the house
evi= the house (direct object of an action)
evde= in the house
evden= from the house

From this you can see what the word "grammar" really means. In these examples it has nothing to do with "correct" speech. It has to do with getting the meaning right. If you use a wrong grammatical ending here, you're not inelegant, you're plain not understood. *The grammar rules are designed to make the relationships among words clear.* That's why we have to pay close attention to the grammar rules of the foreign language we study.

The language you study may not have case endings on the nouns (French, Spanish, Italian, Chinese, for example, don't), but most languages do use some of them. Be prepared for them and try to appreciate why it's so important to get them right.

All of this may be interesting, you say, but it also makes for a lot more work in learning these languages. You're right. But once again let's remember how different people see all these changes. We see German or Russian grammar forcing us into extra labor to demonstrate relationships among words which we English speakers express more simply.

But a Chinese thinks that *our* English grammar rules are a terrible nuisance. He sees us adding "-s" to make a word plural, or having different words for " he" "she" and "it". And "he" changes to "him", "she" changes to "her". He complains that we change all our verbs around from "go" to "went" to "gone", "goes", "going", and so on. Chinese has almost no endings. It just brings in new words to change meaning; perhaps the ultimate in streamlined language. Different strokes for different folks.

Drill, repetition of sentences, use of the material— all of these exercises will make a tremendous difference. It's no good just to learn a list like the one I showed you in Turkish. You've got to hear these endings, practice using them yourself in many different sentences and contexts. They've got to start feeling natural to you—almost second nature. Nothing can replace the tape recorder or classroom drill and conversation practice until you get these endings down cold. If you don't really understand them and feel comfortable with them, it's best not to go on until you do. It's like not digesting a meal properly. It only makes things worse if you go on to eat more on top of an undigested hunk of grammar.

KEY POINTS

1. Grammar is essential because it tells us precisely what the relationship is among words.

2. Many languages, unlike ours, express grammatical relationships among words by means of word endings. For example, something on the end of the word changes to let us know whether the word is the subject or the object of the action.

3. Additional endings may be used on nouns to indicate possession, or location, or motion towards or from the noun.

4. Some languages go in for the use of endings on nouns more thoroughly than others. Russian loves them, German somewhat less, English, French and Chinese, scarcely at all.

5. Use of the wrong ending, that is, bad grammar, is simply confusing because it makes the relationships among the words unclear or it gives an unintended meaning.

CHAPTER TWELVE

THE GENDER GAP (UGH, UGH, UGH)

I promise this will be the last chapter on grammar.
The problem is that you can't really talk about learning a language without tangling with the grammar problem. And it's important that we get a really firm idea of what we're going to encounter before we go sailing off into uncharted waters of a foreign language without a map and some explanation of all the shoals.

This time we're going to talk about a gender gap—one gap that we are probably never going to be able to close.

For some reason or other, in nearly every European language, including French, German, Spanish, Italian, Russian, and even Arabic and Hebrew, there is a curious feature that to our way of thinking is hard to explain. (I've already tried to explain some curious features in other languages that at least have some practical explanation and use. But in this case I have no useful explanation. It's just life...)

Speakers of these languages—starting way back in early history—somehow ended up *categorizing* every single noun in the language into a class of either *masculine, feminine,* and sometimes *neuter.*

OK, so what's unusual about that? We do something of the same in English. "Man, bull, boy, rooster, husband, father", etc., are masculine words in English and we refer to them as "he". Similarly we take words like "girl, daughter, cow, mother, witch" etc., and think of them as feminine, referring to them as "she". And words like "house, car, coal, sky" and so on we think of as having no gender, or neuter, and we refer to them as "it."

Ah, but these European languages *do* categorize words like *house, car, sky, boat, water,* etc as being masculine or feminine. In French and Spanish, for example, *every single noun in the language falls into one of these categories.* In French the words for *house, box, strength, chair, demonstration, glory, street,* and so on are all feminine. The word for "the" with these words is "**la**". But other words like *castle, dog, cake, message, government, paper* and so on are masculine. The word for "the" with these words is always "**le**".

That's not all. When you use an *adjective* with these words like "white paper" or "big street" or "heavy chair", you have to put a *masculine* or *feminine* ending on the adjective to "agree" with the noun. Nuisance? Certainly is, from our point of view. To a Frenchman of course, it comes as naturally as cooking with wine.

Even worse, some languages, German and Russian for example, use all *three* categories—masculine, feminine, *and* neuter. So with each word you have to memorize its grammatical gender. (This is the kind of extra information that you might write down on your word card when you come to memorize the word.) Just as French has *two* different words for "the" depending on whether the word is masculine or feminine, German has *three* different words for "the"—"**der**" "**die**" and "**das**"—for masculine, feminine, and neuter. Russian has *no* word for "the", but you still need to ensure that the corresponding masculine, feminine, or neuter ending is put on any adjective that goes with the noun.

What's more, there is *no logic* about which word falls into which category of grammatical gender. You can't guess from what the word *means* as to whether it is masculine or feminine—unless it is a word like father or mother or boy or girl—and even here there is no guarantee.

Don't blame me. I didn't invent the rules. I'm just trying to prepare you for what's coming up when you start. And just to rub it in, the Chinese think all this gender business is silly and unnecessary anyway. We already mentioned earlier that the Chinese (and Turks, and Persians, and Japanese, among others) find it good enough to use one word for "he", "she", and "it". These are languages without gender gaps.

Don't let all of this discourage you. It may seem strange, or a nuisance at first, but you'll get used to it pretty fast. The good news is that there are even rules in most of these languages which let you guess a good percentage of the time what gender a word happens to be—depending on the letters that it ends in.

In all, this is one gender gap that can't be overcome by legislation. The only way to overcome this one is by memorization. But, as the French say, **Vive la différence!** (In French **différence** is feminine).

KEY POINTS

1. Most European languages categorize every single noun in the language into one of two (masculine and feminine) or one of three (masculine, feminine and neuter) gender categories—regardless of the meaning of the word.

2. The gender of the word often affects the grammatical endings of other, related words.

3. Always learn the gender of each word as you learn the word, perhaps noting it on your word card along with the noun.

CHAPTER THIRTEEN

MOVING OFF PLATEAUS

When you first start your language course, you'll feel that you're making progress rapidly. After all, when you know five words and then learn five more—you've doubled your vocabulary. Alas, this sense of rapid progress doesn't last forever. There will be lulls along the way—what we call plateaus. The first plateau comes when you've passed through the opening phase of language and the novelty of learning has begun to wear off. This is when you're able to hold simple, but real, conversations. Still, there are many more things that you want to say but can't.

Don't be discouraged. No one ever makes constant, consistent progress. We all reach plateaus from time to time when we learn new languages—or when we learn anything else, for that matter. Moreover, time spent on a plateau is really time when your brain is unconsciously consolidating what it has already learned. (I shouldn't tell you this, but sometimes even if you *haven't* been studying your language for a short while, it continues to sink into your brain. So in fact you're making progress even though you're not aware of it.)

Still, you want to get off that plateau as quickly as you can. Here are some things to do that will get you moving forward again:

When you don't know the word for something, find a way to get on without it. If you can't say "he loves music" then say "he likes music very much." If you can't say "she tried to avoid the accident" then say "she didn't want her car to hit the other car." If you're really stuck getting your meaning across, be imaginative. My daughter was in France and got a flat tire. Over the phone to a mechanic she didn't know the word for "flat" so she explained that the tire was "dead." Okay, it's not too elegant. But the mechanic got the point. She communicated.

Learn set phrases and expressions. This is an easy way to expand your repertoire and to help your conversation sound much more fluent:

"What I want to say is..."
"Well, as you may know ..."
"One thing that I want to mention is..."
"You know, it's interesting that..."
"Well, I don't really know, but..."
"It's interesting that you should ask that."
"You know, I was thinking about that earlier."

Of course, you don't want to overdo these phrases, but they give you an idea of how you can stall for time while you're thinking. And they hide awkward pauses.

Go back to some of your earlier lessons and tapes. Listen to them and see how easy it is to repeat them now. This by itself won't get you off your plateau. But it will give you a sense of how far you've come. You'll be surprised.

Look at another textbook on the same language. You will be pleased to see that you already know a

lot of the stuff. You will also find some different be-
ginners' material there that your book didn't have in
the early lessons. You can learn some of this extra
material easily now. And it will probably seem more
fun because it comes more easily and nobody is making
you learn it.

*Buy some kids' books or even comic books in the
language.* You won't understand everything by any
means, but that's not important now. (Comic books,
by the way, are not necessarily easy, either. They often
contain a lot of slang or idiomatic expressions. But you
can learn a few of them and use them—it's often satisfying.)

*Go to a language bookstore and buy a dictionary and
traveler's phrase book of the language.* Just having a
nice new dictionary will help you feel closer to the
language. Look up some words that you found in your
comic book. You don't have to learn them all now—
but again—it helps in making the language feel more
real to you. Also, it's a nice feeling if you've learned
some words and expressions ahead of time, out of class
and on your own. When you finally come to them in
your own textbook, you're ahead of the game.

I said at the outset that learning a foreign language
can be lots of fun. You're probably wondering when
the fun starts. The answer is: right now. Here are some
more things that you can do that will help you to move
forward, but also be interesting in and of themselves.

Turn on a short wave radio. See if you can get broadcasts in the language. Again, don't expect too much
and don't be disappointed if you find that you understand very little of what you hear. It often comes in a
rush later on anyway, when suddenly lots of things
start falling in place. At least listening to the radio and
catching even a few words helps make the language
seem much more "real" and immediate to you.

Go someplace where you can hear the language being spoken, like a foreign grocery store. Try to pick out some words and phrases that sound familiar to you. Warning: don't expect to be able to understand too much of what native speakers are saying to one another. Real comprehension of this kind of conversation will come much later.

Go to a movie that's made in the language you're studying. Make sure that the movie is in the original version, not dubbed into English. If it has subtitles in English—that won't hurt. Again, be prepared for the fact that you won't understand very much at this point. It is actually very hard to understand a foreign film, sometimes just because the sound-track isn't clear. Moreover, movies have a lot of slang in them. (Have you ever seen a British film where you really had to strain to understand what was being said? That's why a foreign- language film is often so hard to understand.)

But this doesn't mean you won't get a lot out of the effort. If you look at the subtitles and then try to catch the same thing from the sound-track, you can learn a lot. But remember, subtitles don't translate everything that's being said on-screen; they give only the gist of the dialogue. Even watching the action and the gestures, and listening to the sounds, will give you a feel for the culture of the language you're studying. Television programs—if you can find any—are often better than movies. Usually people speak more directly into a television camera than they do in films. And the material tends to be more straightforward.

Go to a foreign restaurant. Eat lunch or dinner at some restaurants that serve food from the country whose language you're learning. This by itself will help you feel closer to the language and to its culture. In any case, you'll need to know something about the names of dishes. If your waiter or waitress is a native, try to order in his or her language. At least say "hello" and "thank you". Don't worry about making mistakes;

they'll probably help you and be delighted at your efforts. I've often gotten special service and attention from just such simple efforts. (And you can always leave a generous tip.)

Buy a foreign newspaper. Look at the headlines and see if you can figure out what the words mean. Turn to the section of the paper that interests you the most— sports, fashion, business, or whatever. Read as much as you can, and see if you can at least get the gist of it. Use a dictionary if you need to. The new words you'll learn are bound to come in handy sooner or later.

Grab every occasion to use your language with a foreigner. Using your Chinese on a Korean of course may not win you a lot of points, but the right language with the right native will help a lot. They will really appreciate it. Even if you can only tell them a few simple things, the effort is important. In one more month you can probably tell them more about yourself, and even more after six months.

Above all, when you're on a plateau take every opportunity you can to practice. When native speakers aren't around you should try talking to *yourself* in your new language whenever you have the chance. Walking, jogging, or driving to work are good opportunities. Tell yourself stories, or repeat your dialogues, or invent a conversation with yourself. This is all part of the drill of spending so many hours functioning in the language that it really starts to sink in and become second nature.

Remember again that *time is your friend.* If you keep plugging away you will surely make progress even if it doesn't feel like it.

KEY POINTS

1. Sooner or later you'll reach a plateau. Don't be discouraged. Time will help you.

2. You can help yourself move off the plateau by working to consolidate what you've already learned, and by dipping into the culture a little bit.

3. Practice, practice, practice.

CHAPTER FOURTEEN

HOW FAR CAN YOU REALLY GET?

A language is like an ocean: it seems to go on forever. And it does. How far *you* go depends on your own goals. To be honest with you, it takes years of study to become totally fluent and proficient in a foreign language. The good news is that you don't have to become fluent to start making yourself understood in a foreign language. Even if you're going to take just one course at school, or spend two weeks reading through a language handbook before traveling overseas on holiday or on business, you'll be surprised at how far you can really get.

There are some practical realities about learning a language that you should be aware of. Some types of situations in a language are much harder than others, as you will find out at first-hand. For example, talking one-on-one with another person in a foreign language is always much easier than talking in a group conversation. Why? Because you have much greater control over the conversation when it's just you and the other person.

You'll find that you get fairly familiar with certain kinds of conversations, certain topics that you tend to go over again and again. Topics like where are you from, how long have you been studying Mongolian, how do you like Patagonia, and so on. Even when you're not quite sure whether or not you understood the question you can usually guess what the question was, and give the answer you think is expected.

Be prepared to have to do a good bit of guessing in conversations with foreigners. You get quite good at guessing after a while. Sometimes you might not even catch more than one or two words in a question. It either comes too fast or there are too many words you still don't know. In such cases you have the choice of admitting that you didn't understand and ask for a repeat—or else fake it and guess what the person was driving at.

It's usually best to admit you don't understand, but sometimes you can only say that so many times before you start feeling very awkward. But it can be embarrassing if you guess wrong:

"How long have you been in Jakarta, Mr. Smith?"
"Yes, I do."

"Do you want to visit the electronics factory before dinner?"
"No thank you, I already ate lunch."

Usually a native will speak more slowly and clearly if he knows you're a foreigner in his country. That's a big help and lets you tune in more clearly and listen carefully.

If you are talking with just one other person, you can try to steer the conversation. In fact, you should try to keep some control over the conversation or else it will take unexpected turns that can be very confusing.

Frankly, you will always be doing some degree of guessing at this intermediary stage of the language. You will not know enough words to catch everything and you will have to rely on your wits to handle the conversation.

You will be somewhat more comfortable when you know the topic under discussion. But when the speaker suddenly changes the subject you may have to listen quite hard again to be sure that you've followed the transition to the new topic. As soon as you know the topic you can anticipate a lot of what might be coming up.

Set yourself realistic goals. Don't expect to be able to express yourself like a native. A native speaker is someone who has grown up speaking the language. He will know almost all facets of the language—the slang, the baby words, the jokes, the puns, the rhymes, the formal language, the advertising slogans, the famous literary quotations—everything. Only when you've lived in a country for years and years will you start approximating what a real native speaker can do.

The good news is that you don't have to be a native speaker. You're not trying to sound like you've grown up and lived in that country all your life. You are interested in the practical ability to communicate in the language on everyday matters and on those specialized topics that relate to your personal or professional interests.

What you must do is decide how proficient you want to be and how much time you can devote to that effort. You may find as you get into the language that you enjoy the experience so much that you're willing to devote even more time to it. That's great. And if you're living overseas you'll have even more chance to hear and practice your language.

In the end, practice is the single most important rule for making progress. Remember the old gag, "Excuse me, how do I get to Carnegie Hall?" "Practice, man, practice."

A few words of caution as you set off on your language venture. You aren't going to be able to operate as well outside your classroom as you were in it. Here are some things to be aware of:

Watch out for local accents. You know what a variety of accents we have in America: Brooklyn, Boston, New Jersey, Virginia, Tennessee, Texas, Iowa, and so on. Well, foreign countries are that way too. Even small countries can have a bewildering mixture of regional accents. England has far more differences per square mile than the US.

Be prepared for the fact that not everybody is going to talk like your language teacher, like your language tape, or like a radio announcer. You will run across country bumpkin types, authentic mushmouths, mumblers, down-home drawlers, machine gun motor mouths and everything else. Most languages will have strong regional dialects. It's tough at first. But with time it will get better as your ear learns to tune in a little more closely and grow accustomed to a variety of regional accents. For example, you'll be able to tell that your conversation partner is from Southern France or Northern Italy.

Beware of the telephone. Sooner or later you will have to pick up the phone or put in a call to somebody when you're in a foreign country. Be prepared for the worst. What's so bad about it? The main problem is you can't see the mouth of the person talking.

You may not realize it, but we depend a lot on our eyes when we listen to people talk. We actually lip read to some extent—especially as we strain to follow someone speaking in a foreign language. On the telephone we are handicapped because we can't see the mouth of the speaker. On top of that, the sound of the phone is never as clear as it is in a face-to-face conversation. And everyone seems to speak awfully fast.

Beware of jokes. Anyone who has ever had much experience at learning a language will tell you that jokes are an area of sudden death for the intermediate language student. The problem is that jokes, by definition, depend on plays on words or sudden surprise turns in a story. And, by definition, this is the one area you are least prepared for. I've never found a satisfactory way out of this bind. Usually I end up following most of the story until they get to the punch line—and then I muff it.

You can try to laugh at a joke anyway. But I often find that I laugh before the real punch line comes. Or I wait too long and don't laugh when the joke is over. Just take it from me that jokes are usually bad news. But as you get better in the language, jokes can offer you unique kinds of insights into the life of the country you're studying.

Don't cuss. Every language has its cuss words. And every kid growing up learns pretty fast that it's not so much the words themselves that are are important, but the company that you use them in. When you're out with friends or close colleagues your own age, chances are you're going to use some words that you would avoid using in front of your parents or your own kids.

It's the same thing with a foreign language, only more so. Your teacher or a foreign friend might teach you some choice swear words, but you use them at your peril. Perhaps you've heard foreigners swear in English when they don't know the language very well. Usually it sounds terrible. You've heard the words a thousand times, but they use them in the wrong situation, or don't fully understand the impact of the word. Remember there is a fine line among swear words. Which word is worse than another is something that usually only a person who knows a language very well can determine. It will take you quite some time to know exactly what word you can use when and with whom. Until you really know that, best stay away from using them.

If you have a fairly good experience learning your first foreign language, you might be tempted to try another. If so, you'll find that each new language gets easier to learn. You become more familiar with the way languages work. You notice similarities among words that help you remember them better. You know more about the "tricks" of language study.

That's what this book has been all about. Showing you what I've learned along the way as I've studied one language after another. If I've succeeded, by now you should have a good idea of what to expect when you start to learn a foreign language, and of how to approach the task.

Finally, I hope I've imparted to you some sort of my own enthusiasm for the rewards that learning a new language brings. An old Chinese proverb says "One language, one man; two languages, two men." In effect when you learn a new language you become a new person, with a new culture, and even a new way of looking at things. Your whole perspective on the outside world changes.

So, good luck. And don't forget to have some fun along the way.

SPECIAL SECTION

GOING IT ALONE

Can you learn a language by yourself? Yes, indeed! It's not easy, but it can definitely be done. I've learned a few that way myself.

If you're seriously interested in learning a language on your own, then this book is especially important to you. It contains the kinds of pointers that otherwise only a teacher could give you. Let's go over the special types of problems that you will need to look out for, and talk about how to solve them.

The problem of incentive: Obviously, you already have a good bit of incentive if you're interested in going forward on your own. You clearly know what you want: either you're planning to go on a trip, or to live in a foreign country or the language means a lot to you. Or maybe you just have a lot of intellectual curiosity.

The chapter on what to do when you start feeling stuck on a plateau will be especially relevant. You are going to need extra help in maintaining motivation, so foreign films, foreign foods, foreign friends, music, books, comics, radio broadcasts or whatever, will be especially useful to you.

You'll need good language materials. Good materials always help, but if you don't have a teacher they are imperative. Try to find someone to ask about a good textbook, especially if you haven't had much exposure to language study before. A lot of famous language schools have textbooks commercially available, and they often come with tapes.

You should make it a point to buy several different textbooks. This can help you in several ways. You will have a variety of materials to help explain things to you more fully. Any language book will have its own strengths and weaknesses so if you have several, you get the benefit of different explanations and viewpoints on the same skills. In addition, you will find it a refreshing break to go over to another textbook just as a change of routine. When you get bogged down in one, switch to another.

The need for tapes will be absolutely critical if you are on your own. You can either find them on the market, or you can find somebody somewhere who is a native speaker of the language who can make some tapes for you. You can't do without tapes if you're on your own. You just can't.

Find native speakers. You will have to have some contact with native speakers if you don't have a formal teacher. If you live near a university, go and ask at the relevant language department. They can probably tell you whether there are foreign students around who might be willing to help you out—either for free, for a small fee, or in exchange for some help in English. If you can arrange it, this last way is best of all since it will give you a lot more opportunity to find out more about the language and culture you're interested in.

If you aren't near a university, try churches or religious groups from the country of your interest. Or grocery stores from that country where you could ask about native speakers or maybe leave a small want-ad asking for some help from a native speaker. Remember, the native speaker can not only help make the language alive and more fun, but can also help you with any problems you may encounter—and can become a *real* friend.

You may want to learn only how to *read* a foreign language, and not get involved in learning to speak or understand the spoken language. This is often the case for people who are interested in using the language as a research tool.

I personally feel that you're missing a lot of the fun and the rare experience of the foreign language if you limit yourself just to reading it. But even learning to read has its challenges—and you still can learn a lot about the culture and the mental processes involved in the language. But even if you are only interested in learning to read, it's still important to learn to *think* in the language. Remember, you don't want to have to translate as you read. Translating is time-consuming and inefficient. You will need to be able to read just as a native of the language would read—straight from the language to the concept in your head—no intermediary process.

So it will still be crucial to spend a little time with tapes to rev up your thinking processes in your new language. Make sure you read out loud a lot, and try to understand what you read without translating. You'll never be an accomplished reader in the language if you have to translate.

If you are learning only how to read, make sure that in addition to the regular textbooks you also get a proper reader—a book with graduated reading passages and vocabulary, designed to give you practice in reading. There is just no substitute for getting such a book. There are some very good readers on the market today, in particular those produced by the Foreign Service Institute of the US State Department. Their books are available from the US Government Printing Office.

The main feature of these good readers is that they let you read great quantities of "controlled" material written with just the words you know at every stage. That way you become comfortable at reading extensively—getting heavy repetition of the material you're studying. Beware of books that don't give you much opportunity to practice and reinforce the material you've learned. I'd buy every reader I could get my hands on just to ensure that I had every opportunity to repeat and repeat in different contexts.

There is no reason why you can't learn a language on your own. It is a heavy undertaking, but a challenging and exciting one. You'll just have to pay extra attention to the problems of keeping up your incentive and getting your hands on good language materials.

You'll also need to establish some contact with a native speaker. But when you work on your own, you know exactly why you're doing it. You can push yourself that much harder. You will be your own harshest critic—and that can make the rewards of success all the more satisfying.